criollo dark
conching # A passion for
chocolate pot # chocolate
truffle indulgence
creamy

Dominique Ayral

CASSELL&CO

 **million**
tonnes of cocoa are produced on the Ivory Coast.

80 cargas, or 3.84 million cocoa beans were paid by Cihuatlan province to the king twice a year. The annual taxes levied on the whole Aztec territory amounted to 100 tonnes of cocoa beans.

With a cocoa content higher than 75%, chocolate can taste too bitter, particularly if the beans used are high quality, or if they have been poorly dried or roasted.

fl.65 billion

turnover for the cocoa industry ranks it third in world food commodities after sugar and coffee. ▶ 66

2.6 million

tonnes of cocoa are produced worldwide. ▶ 66

35 pods a year

is the average yield of a cacao tree. The fruits grow straight out of the trunk and main branches. The tree thrives in the hot, humid climate of tropical forests.

 68

5 % vegetable fats

other than cocoa butter have been permitted to be added since 15 March, 2000. Whatever the purists may say, in the eyes of the law it is therefore still chocolate.

 104

2.65 kg

filled chocolate bars

per person per year are eaten in the United States. The filled chocolate bar was invented at the beginning of the 20th century. ▶ 89

Among the world's favourite chocolate products, did you know that **Nutella** *(chocolate hazelnut spread) and* **Mon Chéri** *are of Italian origin, or that* **Toblerone** *is Swiss?*

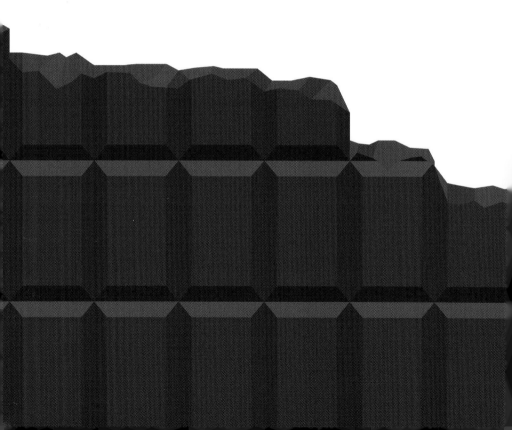

Chocolate *can be plain, milk or white (a blend of cocoa butter, sugar and milk).*

 110

In the Aztec empire

cocoa beans, the seeds found in the pods of a cacao tree, were used as **currency**, and to pay certain **taxes**. Depending on the rate at the time, a rabbit cost between 4 and 10 beans, the services of a prostitute 10 to 12 beans and a slave a princely 100 cocoa beans. ▶ 17

In 1674, chocolate was sold as a solid product for the first time. It was available in a London shop, At the Coffee Mill and Tobacco Roll, in 'Spanish cake' and in pastille form. A number of European chocolatiers copied the recipe.

26

British, Americans and Spanish like it very sweet. The Japanese are developing a taste for it and, like the French, prefer it to be bitter.

78

During the long expeditions to conquer the New World, chocolate replaced water and wine. Cortés remarked that 'just one glass was sufficient to refresh a soldier for the whole day'. Chocolaterías were introduced and stayed open all day.

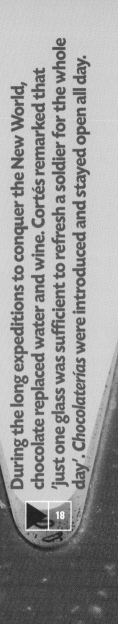 18

What is the effect of chocolate? A feeling of contentment and an overwhelming blissful euphoria, or so say some fanatics. What is the scientific cause? The chemical anandamide, a neurotransmitter, which has similar effects to cannabis.

45

Perceived in Britain as **a remedy**, chocolate

became **a nutritional supplement** for the

public (in particular labourers and children).

Recognised **today** as a **stress-reliever** and

pick-me-up because of the minerals it contains

(such as magnesium, potassium) and the alkaloid

salsolinol, chocolate is a source of **daily**

goodness . ▶ 45

An excellent chocolate with a **55 % cocoa content** tastes far better than a poor chocolate with **70 %.**

DISCOVER

IN 1519, HERNAN CORTÉS LANDED IN THE NEW WORLD.
HAILED AS A GOD BY KING MONTEZUMA II AND HIS PEOPLE,
WHO BELIEVED HIM TO BE THE MYTHICAL QUETZALCOATL,
HE WAS OFFERED *XOCOATL*, OR CHOCOLATE.
TODAY THE SACRED DRINK OF THE AZTECS HAS BECOME
POPULAR THE WORLD OVER.

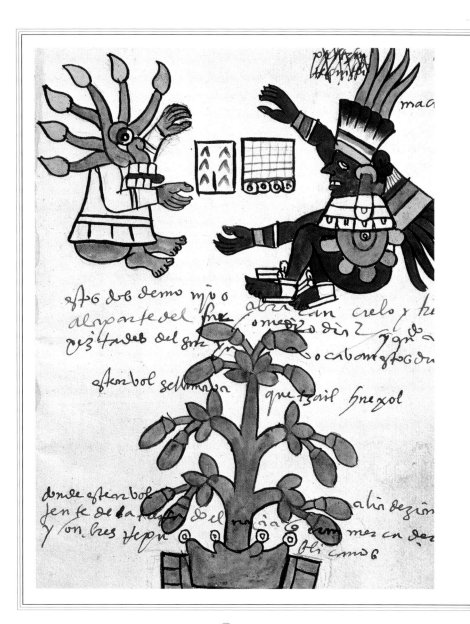

esto dxe demo mjo o
al oparte del fue   abrian crelo y ti
cestades del gra   omexo diz Z gra a
                        o cabon esto du

este arbol se llamava   quetzal huexol

donde esta arbol   alin dezin
jen te de la regia del mucia to temes en de
y con. bres tepu   oliamo s

According to the legend, in the heart of the rainforest that lay between the Orinoco and the Amazon, there grew a tree with a silvery-grey bark. Being a tender species, it would always take root in the shade of taller trees to protect itself from the scorching sun. When it was mature, buds, flowers and large orange-brown fruits grew directly from its trunk and branches. The monkeys and parrots living in the forest would pick the ripest fruits, crack their shells and eat their pulpy contents. One day an Indian out looking for food saw the animals and decided to take a look at the fruit himself. When he opened one, he saw that as well as the pulp, it contained large seeds. At first he didn't know what to do with the seeds, until one day, he saw that they had begun to dry out, having been left lying in the sun all day. As an experiment, he tried one, and although it was quite bitter, he nonetheless found that he liked the taste. So began our great love affair with chocolate.

THE LEGEND OF QUETZALCOATL

In the region that would later become known as Central America, to the south of present-day Mexico, ruled the great civilisation of the Mayas. Their leader, King Hunahpu, ordered his people to cultivate the cacoa tree in order to make a ceremonial drink called *chaucau haa*. By the 10th century AD, the Mayan empire was in decline and eventually gave way to the Toltecs, who were ruled by their great King Quetzalcoatl. He kept a huge garden near his home town of Tula, to the north of present-day Mexico City, where he would gather flowers for the gods and harvest fruits for his people. Quetzacoatl revered the cacao tree and learned how to cultivate it, believing that its beans could soothe pain and stimulate the mind.

THE AZTECS

Cocoa comes from cacahuatl, a substance derived from cacahuaquahuitl, the cacao tree of Quetzalcoatl, known as the Feathered Serpent, King of the Toltecs.

The Toltec era was a golden age and the kingdom was peaceful until internal struggles forced Quetzacoatl to flee the country accompanied by his followers. However, before leaving he vowed that he would return in the year of the *ce-acalt* (a reed in the Toltec language) to reclaim his kingdom and would bring with him all the treasures of Paradise for his people to enjoy.

The years passed and the Toltecs began to worship their departed king, Quetzalcoatl, as a god of soil fertility, representing him as a feathered serpent. They continued the cultivation of the cacao tree and all the rituals that were associated with it. They chose the best seeds for new plantations, leaving them in the moonlight for four nights to make them fertile. When the Toltecs were in turn conquered by the Aztecs at the beginning of the 14th century the conquerors took over many of their traditions, including in particular how to produce the *xocoatl* or 'cocoa of the land'. Holding heavy sticks, they performed the 'cocoa dance', hammering

out an incessant rhythm on the newly harvested pods. After the ritual the split pods were left to ferment where they lay, so that the pulp protecting the cocoa beans gradually disappeared, leaving behind the beans, which were then washed in fresh water and left to dry in the sun. As a further purifying process, they were roasted to stop mould from forming. When all unwanted fibres had been removed, the cocoa beans were crushed on flat stones until they were reduced to a coarse powder. This was then moulded into a kind of cake from which pieces were removed to make the *xocoatl*. Only the king, priests, princes, higher officials and the richest merchants were allowed to drink this beverage, and the wealthier the dignitary, the more complex the recipe. Pepper, vanilla, pimento, cinnamon, musk and maize could all be added to the basic mixture of cocoa mass and water, which had been vigorously whipped into a froth to draw off the fat.

COCOA BEANS BECOME A CURRENCY

The Aztecs planted cacao trees from southern Mexico to Guatemala, but the planting was too sparse and their production was small, so cocoa beans remained a rare commodity. As a result of their scarcity they became a currency, as they had been in Mayan times. The rich would use some cocoa beans to make *xocoatl* and kept the rest for transactions. To buy a rabbit would cost from four to ten cocoa beans; the services of a prostitute would cost ten to twelve beans, while a slave would cost a hundred. Tributes measured in *cargas* (one *carga* was equivalent to 24,000 cocoa beans, or a load of 25 to 30 kg/55 to 66 lb) were levied on all new cocoa plantations. The province of Cihuatlan, on the Pacific coast, had to pay the king 80 *cargas*, or 3,840,000 cocoa beans, twice a year. In total the annual tax levied on the whole Aztec territory amounted to 100 tonnes of cocoa beans.

THE TREASURE OF COCOA

Ek Chuah, depicted on this 12th- or 13th-century manuscript with a black face, was the god of commerce and cocoa. Cocoa was also used as a currency for trade and for taxes.

Life moved peacefully with the rhythm of the seasons, revolving around the harvests of their precious, magical beans. However, at the end of July 1502 Christopher Columbus moored the *Santa Maria* just off the island of Guanaja, near the coast of Honduras. Dressed in ceremonial splendour, the Aztecs sailed in a huge boat to meet the strange visitor and present him with gifts, among them a sack filled to the brim with cocoa beans. Seeing they were valuable to the Aztecs, Christopher Columbus gave them a few of his wares in exchange and was held in great esteem.

However, when the Indians offered him their sacred drink, he took one sip and immediately spat it straight out. He was nauseated by the bitter, spicy gruel and could see no reason to take cocoa back home with him.

THE RETURN OF QUETZALCOATL

In 1519 an enormous ship loomed over the horizon on the coast of Tabasco. As it came nearer, thousands of lights seemed to sparkle from it. Men dressed in plumed helmets and shining armour, which reflected the rays of the sun, were crowded on to the decks, waiting to disembark. It dawned on the petrified Aztecs that this was indeed the year of the *ce-acatl*, when their lost king, Quetzalcoatl, had promised to return to his people. Standing at of the head of two great dugout canoes, the current Aztec king Montezuma set off to welcome the legendary god back to his former kingdom. However, what the Aztecs did not realise was that it was not Quetzacoatl in a plumed helmet on board the ship, but Hernan Cortés, the conquistador, who had come to colonise the New World. The Aztec people hailed him as a god and showered him with gold and precious objects. Not wishing to disappoint them, Cortés strode off regally in the direction of the capital Tenochtitlán. Montezuma believed that this was the fulfilment of the prophecy of his ancestors, and proclaimed: 'You are the very men our fathers said would return from the land of the rising sun. You will have all that you need since this is your homeland.' With that, the king offered Cortés a cacao tree plantation as a tribute, and invited him to attend a banquet boasting all the riches of the Aztec people. At the end of the meal *xocoatl* was served in goblets of solid gold. As he watched the assembled people, Cortés noticed that all the dignitaries were

LIVING LEGEND

When Hernan Cortés landed in South America, he was greeted by the Aztec Emperor, King Montezuma II, who thought he was witnessing the return of Quetzalcoatl, the much revered mythical god-king.

drinking it in large quantities. He learned that Montezuma drank it daily and that his secret stores of powder were closely guarded in golden boxes, and he wondered why it was considered to be so important. The conquistador discovered that *xocoatl* was said to be both an aphrodisiac and a tonic, and that cocoa butter was used both during religious ceremonies and to make ointment for soothing burns.

COCOA FOR SPANISH TASTES

Even if it was not to his taste, Cortés recognised the value of cocoa beans. He began to organise the cultivation of the cacao tree from Mexico to Trinidad and as far as Haiti. He sweetened the *xocoatl* recipe by adding honey, and during the long expeditions to conquer the New World, chocolate replaced wine, which was still rarely found in this promised land. Cortés remarked that 'just one glass was enough to refresh a soldier for the whole day'. *Chocolaterías* began to open, serving chocolate all day long. It was prepared mostly as a hot drink, boiling water being poured straight on to a mixture of cocoa mass and spices, which made the cocoa butter rise to

the surface. The liquid was then whisked into a froth and sweetened with honey. Later, the honey was replaced by sugar, which was brought from the sugar cane plantations of Mexico and Saint Domingo. The chocolate was flavoured with aniseed, almonds or hazelnuts and orange blossom, and was served with slices of bread or biscuits.

Xocoatl had changed greatly since it was discovered by the Mayas. Even if its method of preparation was still somewhat rudimentary, the time had come for its passage across the Atlantic to the Spanish court of Charles V and the subsequent conquest of Europe.

COCOA AND THE LADIES OF THE SPANISH NOBILITY

In 1527 Hernan Cortés returned to Spain. Among his belongings he carried with him cocoa beans and all the equipment needed to make chocolate. However, Charles V paid it little attention, and the only people to show an interest were the botanists. As time went on and more colonists returned, *xocoatl* began to find some favour among the Spanish. Most of the demand came from convents and monasteries, because chocolate had become the official drink taken during long periods of fasting. In 1585 the first cargo arrived in Seville from Veracruz.

THE TRAPPINGS OF CHOCOLATE

Chocolate-drinking was even depicted on fabrics and tapestries in the houses of Spanish aristocrats.

This was the beginning of the cocoa trade. It was accepted by the aristocracy, and the ladies at court took a quite exceptional interest in it. Excited by the claim that the seeds used to make this healthy, nourishing drink promoted fertility, they would meet at the end of the afternoon to partake in a new ritual – drinking chocolate. Teams of chambermaids would bring bowls filled with sugar cane, milk and eggs and place them on pedestal tables. The ladies could then choose whether or not to add some of these ingredients to the spicy, hot, brown liquid, which was brought to them in a chocolate pot. Standing on a tripod and made preferably from copper, this vessel, shaped like a bulb towards its base, had a spout and a horizontal handle to prevent scalding. There was a hole in the centre of the lid to allow the insertion of a stirring stick or whisk. Advances in culinary techniques brought about the creation of exquisitely elegant objects. Precious materials, such as gold, silver, porcelain and silver gilt, were chosen. They were engraved, inlaid or decorated with delicate motifs. Porcelain cups standing on finely crafted saucers were slowly filled with liberal helpings of chocolate. For an even greater appreciation of this agreeable drink, a new cup, known as the 'trembleuse', was invented, which had a well in the saucer for maximum stability.

Great quantities of chocolate were drunk at these social gatherings – 'as much as stomachs could hold'– and the whole Spanish empire was prepared to defend its cocoa plantations to the death in response to this craze from the New World. The Spanish monopoly of the cocoa trade, along with the Spanish recipe for drinking chocolate, was to last for more than a century.

CHOCOLATE ARRIVES IN FRANCE AND ITALY

On his return from a voyage to trade with the American colonies in 1606, Antonio Carletti introduced the precious drink into Italy. Turin, Perugia and Venice became shrines to Italian chocolate. At the same time *cioccolateri* (chocolatiers or chocolate makers) began the tradition of touring local markets, where they prepared a wonderfully exotic, gooey, brown brew for passers-by. Cocoa arrived in France anonymously in 1609 when, during the dark days of the Inquisition, Portuguese and Spanish Jews were forced to seek asylum in Bayonne, close to the Spanish border and one of the Atlantic ports open to refugees. A good many of them were chocolatiers by trade, and they set up workshops, to the great delight of the people of Bayonne who were the first to sample cocoa before it had even arrived at the royal court of France. In 1615, under the terms of a peace treaty between the two nations, Anne of Austria, eldest daughter of Philip II of Spain, was betrothed to the French Prince Louis XIII, son of Henri IV and Marie de Médicis. Anne of Austria brought with her a team of attendants, one of whom was called the *molina*. She was in charge of the ingredients used in chocolate making, and it was her task to prepare and whip the chocolate using a whisk, or *molinillo*. One of the first aristocrats to express a liking for Spanish chocolate was the Cardinal of Lyon, Alphonse de Richelieu. He became a dedicated enthusiast when his melancholia instantly lifted at the first mouthful. Soon his brother Armand Jean du Plessis, the famous Cardinal Richelieu, also fell to the delights of chocolate after his doctor recommended a daily dose, as did Anne of Austria's lover, Cardinal Mazarin. For some years the enjoyment of chocolate was confined to the small circle of close associates of the queen, and the people of Bayonne. It was only after 1660 and the marriage of Marie-Therese of Austria – another Spanish infanta – to Louis XIV that chocolate became more widespread. The Sun King was not particularly taken by chocolate, but he nevertheless gave his permission for a merchant named David Caillou to market it 'in all the towns and other places in this kingdom that would seem appropriate to him, be it in liquor or pastille form, in boxes or in any other manner that he should see fit'. Caillou became the only chocolate merchant in Paris, and in 1671 he opened the first drinking chocolate shop on the Rue de l'Arbre-Sec. It was there that he is said to have devised a new manufacturing process, crushing the roasted cocoa beans twice, the second time with a heavy iron roller. This produced a much finer powder, from which it was possible to make a much smoother drink.

BAYONNE

Chocolate made its first appearance in France in Bayonne, which is close to the Spanish border and was one of the few cities to offer refuge to Jews fleeing from the Inquisition. They were masters of processing cocoa.

THE END OF SPAIN'S MONOPOLY

The Spanish monopoly of the cocoa trade was broken after conflicts with both the English, who wished to extend their empire, and the Dutch, who were pushing for independence. The English seized Jamaica from the Spanish, and began to import cocoa into London. Following the arrival in 1657 of a French chocolatier in the city, an advertisement in the *Public Advertiser* declared that 'in Bishopsgate St, in Queen's Head Alley, at a Frenchman's house, is an excellent West Indian drink called Chocolate to be sold, where you can have it ready at any time, and also unmade at reasonable rates'. This was followed by the introduction of new types of club, chocolate houses and coffee houses, which made chocolate available not only to the English aristocracy but also, as a new departure, to the middle classes. The best-known chocolate houses were the Cocoa Tree, and White's, which became a famous gentleman's club. The number of voyages to the New World increased. Every country wanted its piece of El Dorado, maritime transport improved, and the cocoa trade flourished. Throughout the 17th century chocolate was renowned as a health food as scientists discovered more of its benefits. Having passed a largely drunken evening, the diarist Samuel Pepys wrote: 'Waked in the morning, with my head in a sad taking through the last night's drink, which I am very sorry for; so rose, and went out with Mr Creed to drink our morning draught, which he did give me in chocolate to settle my stomach.' Still largely unknown in the provinces, the consumption of chocolate remained peculiar to cities and ports and continued to be a privilege enjoyed only by society's élite. Its texture, taste and consistency were improved, but chocolate was nevertheless still available only in the form of a cocoa mass to which were added cinnamon, cloves and sugar. More sophisticated recipes suggested the addition of an egg yolk or Madeira. The preference in Italy was to flavour it with either sweet jasmine or sharp citron, whereas some German noblemen liked to dissolve it in wine. It was an English doctor, Sir Hans Sloane, who recommended drinking it sweetened, with hot milk. As personal physician to the Duke of Albermarle, Governor of Jamaica, Sloane spent two years in the West Indies and on his return, began to import and manufacture cocoa. This he recommended should be drunk with hot milk and honey 'for its Lightness on the Stomach'. Chocolate was promoted for the treatment of consumption and stomach troubles, and Sloane's cocoa was advertised as being 'Greatly recommended by several eminent Physicians'. Pierre Masson, a café owner by trade, set out a recipe for drinking chocolate in his book, 'The perfect café owner, or how to make tea, coffee, chocolate and other hot and cold

THE END OF A MONOPOLY

A cocoa plantation on the island of Grenada. Spain finally lost its monopoly on cocoa cultivation and production. Other nations wanted a slice of the chocolate cakes too.

liquors'. 'If you want to make milk chocolate take as much milk as you would normally take water ..., boil it, and make sure that it does not turn sour or boil over; remove it from the heat and add as much sugar and chocolate as before ... Having poured everything into the chocolate pot stir it well into a froth with a stick, and serve.' Solid chocolate was sold for the first time in 1674. A London shop, At the Coffee Mill and Tobacco Roll, sold it as a 'Spanish cake' or in pastille form. The appeal of this product was so great that a number of European chocolatiers also began to make it. As countries became more economically, politically and culturally developed, so chocolate was established as a desirable luxury.

BIRTH OF AN INDUSTRY

Cocoa mass did not keep well. At the beginning of the 18th century guidelines were introduced to control its usage. There was a recommendation that it should be used within three months, after which mould or insect infestation could appear and the cocoa butter would turn rancid. In many respects, the manufacture of chocolate was very rudimentary. Small producers still used an archaic technique more or less reminiscent of the original Aztec methods. Conditions were difficult for the workers, who had to rely on their own strength to crush the cocoa beans either manually or with an iron cylinder. It was not until 1732 that a Frenchman named Dubuisson marketed a flat table, heated by charcoals on which cocoa beans could be ground while standing rather than kneeling on the floor.

FROTHY CHOCOLATE
Italian noblemen in a café. The delicious chocolate drink was prepared in a bulbous chocolate pot equipped with a whisk for mixing.

In Britain a hydraulic press was introduced to crush the cocoa beans by machine rather than by hand. The first English chocolate factory opened in 1728, using a water-powered engine to process the cocoa beans. It was bought by Joseph Fry some years later. In 1765 the first chocolate factory in America was founded at Dorchester, Massachusetts, by John Hannon and Dr James Baker, and it used a water mill to grind the beans. In the 1780s the first machine-made chocolate was produced in Barcelona, but the development of the chocolate manufacturing industry made slow progress due to a succession of international conflicts. From 1765 Britain and America were fighting the War of Independence, and the Revolution in France in 1789 led to the Napoleonic Wars in Europe.

PEACE BRINGS EXPERIMENTATION

Drinking chocolate had one big problem. As soon as it cooled and was left to stand, the liquid separated and particles of cocoa dropped to the bottom of the chocolate pot. It was a Dutchman, Coenraad van Houten, who was to find a solution to the problem, experimenting in

the mill that he had converted into a chocolate factory. In 1828 he invented a hydraulic press that facilitated the removal of cocoa butter. Once the extraction was complete, a compressed cake remained, which could then be pulverized into a powder. In 1828 King William I of Holland granted Van Houten the patent for his invention of cocoa powder, and some years later it was again Van Houten who introduced dutching which increased the powder's solubility. This resulted in the first instant chocolate drinks, and combined with a reduced tax on cocoa, chocolate now became available to the general public. An advertisement in *The Poor Man's Guardian* of 10 November 1832 advertised 'THEOBROMA! – J. Cleave begs to call the attention of his Friends and the general Public to the above new beverage, sold only by him, at 2d per pint. Its balsamic and nutritious properties render it peculiarly wholesome, and its cheapness advantageous to the working classes.'

QUALITY SWISS CHOCOLATE

It was relatively late, not until 1750, that the Swiss discovered chocolate via the Italians. However, they quickly made up for lost time and by the 19th century had formulated the recipe for chocolate as we know it today. In 1819, after four years of training in Italy, Jean-Louis Cailler returned to Switzerland and founded a factory at Vevey on the shores of Lake Geneva. He perfected the stone grinding mill that he had been using in Italy to crush and combine the cocoa and sugar, and in 1830 brought out a range of chocolate varieties such as 'pure Caracas' and 'medium sweet'. His customers now had an exciting choice of several products. Encouraged by this success, Charles-Amédée Kohler joined in the adventure, and in 1831 created hazelnut chocolate in his Lausanne factory.

SOLID MILK CHOCOLATE AT LAST

In 1866 Joseph Fry made the first blocks of eating chocolate, from cocoa liquor, sugar and cocoa butter, but chocolate-makers throughout Europe were trying to find a process in which they could combine cocoa power with milk to produce bars of milk chocolate. However, Henri Nestlé in Switzerland had just formulated dried milk powder, and in the United States at roughly the same time condensed milk was invented. The result of combining the two was a milk chocolate bar called 'Gala-Peter', which Nestlé developed in 1875 thanks to these technical innovations. His labours were rewarded at the international exhibition in Paris in 1878, when he was awarded a diploma.

A few years later Jean Tobler, a chocolate merchant, opened his own chocolate factory in Berne in Switzerland. In 1899 he launched

BIRTH OF AN INDUSTRY
From the beginning of the 19th century cocoa beans were no longer laboriously crushed by hand. Chocolate making was mechanised, allowing production to increase to meet demand.

chocolate bars under the brand name Tobler, the most popular bar of which he called Toblerone, a special blend of cocoa and almonds, and, as all chocolate-lovers know, it is still going strong today.

It was another man from Switzerland, Rodolfe Lindt, who was largely responsible for pushing chocolate to the height of luxury. In 1879 he invented 'conching', the re-addition of cocoa butter to the cocoa mass (the crushed and ground cocoa beans) followed by a prolonged kneading process. This gave the chocolate a glossy, velvety smoothness and lessened its acidity.

CHOCOLATE FOR EVERYONE: THE PROMISE OF A BETTER LIFE

Despite the technical advances and the growth of cocoa cultivation, chocolate remained an expensive commodity. This was because, being imported as a luxury product, it was subject to a high level of taxation. Some chocolatiers wanted to make it affordable to everyone, however, and in 1824 John Cadbury opened a grocer's shop in Birmingham, selling drinking chocolate and cocoa among other things. This was so successful that in 1831 he became a manufacturer, establishing his factory in an old malthouse. The Cadbury family were Quakers and, as nonconformists, were barred from the universities and therefore from the professions. This explains the entry of many Quaker families of the day into business – including the chocolate manufacturers Frys, Rowntrees and Terrys. By 1842 John Cadbury was selling 16 sorts of drinking chocolate and 11 cocoas. The business was very much a family one, including John's brother, nephew, and later his sons. The company went from strength

MENIER, THE PHILANTHROPIST

Menier owned cacao plantations in South America and established a factory in Noisiel, France, where he built a village for his employees.

to strength, and in the mid-1850s Prime Minister William Gladstone boosted the market when he reduced taxes on imported cocoa beans, allowing manufacturers to reduce their prices and offer their products more widely. In 1854 Cadburys received the accolade of a Royal Warrant, as 'manufacturers of cocoa and chocolate to Queen Victoria'.

John Cadbury retired in 1861, handing over the reins to his two sons. Although aged only 25 and 21 when they took over the company, Richard and John Cadbury gave the company a new lease of life – the quality of the products was improved, and the business prospered. A huge step forward in British cocoa manufacturing was made by the brothers in 1866. Until then, potato flour or sago had been added to chocolate to absorb excess cocoa butter. But in Holland van Houten had developed a cocoa press to extract the cocoa butter, and the Cadbury brothers followed suit, acquiring a press for their own factory. Cadburys could now market their products as 'Absolutely Pure – Therefore Best', and business boomed. This move also resulted in a new Act of Parliament, the Adulteration of Foods Act (1872 and 1878). Another side-effect was

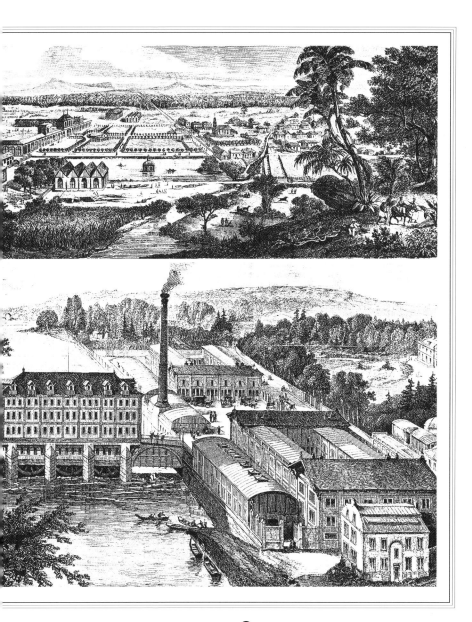

the development of new kinds of eating chocolate, utilising the cocoa butter produced by the pressing process. The growth of the business forced the Cadbury brothers to make a move to bigger premises – they purchased the Bournbrook Estate, 14½ acres of land just outside Birmingham, and built a new factory there. In 1879 production commenced at Bournville, as it was named – 'Bourn' after the estate, and 'ville' meaning 'town', chosen to give a French flavour, because at the time French chocolate had the highest reputation. With the employment of a master confectioner, known affectionately as 'Frederic the Frenchman', Cadburys went on to expand their product range considerably.

Quakers are known for their concern for social welfare, and the Cadbury family were no exception. They were the first firm to introduce a five-and-a-half day working week, they pioneered bank holiday factory closures, and gave their employees time off to attend night school. In 1866 they introduced morning prayers and Bible readings. The factory grounds included sports fields (Richard and George Cadbury were both keen cricketers themselves) and swimming pools. The workers were taken on regular works outings. George Cadbury was largely responsible for the famous Bournville village. He bought 120 acres with the aim of providing affordable housing in pleasant surroundings for Cadbury workers and others, along the lines of the 'Garden City' movement of the time.

CHOCOLATE PATISSERIE

Pastry cooks seized the opportunity to use this new ingredient with so many delicious possibilities in their cakes, ices and desserts.

In the United States Hershey followed suit in 1900, when he disposed of his caramel factory for a princely $1 million and relaunched himself as a chocolate manufacturer. 'Caramels are a fad,' he declared, 'chocolate is a permanent thing.' He created Hersheyville, a model town designed along the lines of Bournville. He was the first to add vegetable fat to chocolate, resulting in a product that, even in the height of summer, did not melt and could be sent to American soldiers as a war ration.

EUROPEAN EXPANSION

As the 19th century progressed, chocolate gradually became available to more and more people through the industrialisation of its manufacturing processes, but it was still perceived as a great luxury and comfort food. The French were major consumers as well as manufacturers; however, at the beginning of the 20th century they were hit head-on by the increasing success of other chocolate-producing nations. In a free market, Menier was forced to shut up shop, and the Swiss company Nestlé was quick to snap the company up. While the Swiss were leaders in creativity, the Germans were smashing records for cocoa imports. In 1913 their chocolate factories numbered more than 200. Thanks to van Houten's cocoa powder and the chocolate in block form invented by Fry in Britain in 1866, chocolate began to be used in cooking. In 1912 the Belgian Jean Neuhaus invented the individual, bite-sized chocolate, filled with various soft centres (almond, nougat and fruit-flavoured creams known as ganache). By way of contrast, Forrest Mars invented the filled chocolate bar in America in 1925. It was these two innovations that resulted in the vast range of chocolate confectionery that we know today.

FIRM FAVOURITES THAT HAVE STOOD THE TEST OF TIME

The 20th century saw a huge increase in the number and variety of different chocolate products, many of which remain firm favourites to this day. Cadbury's Dairy Milk was first produced in 1905 and today it remains the most popular moulded chocolate bar in Britain, with sales of over 250 million bars a year. The recipe remains virtually unchanged to this day. Cadbury's Fruit and Nut, another perennial favourite, appeared in 1923, as did the Milky Way. In 1932 the Mars Bar appeared. The slogan 'A Mars a day helps you work, rest and play' is well known. Black Magic, which was introduced in 1933, is one of the

DRINK OF THE GODS
A Mexican woman prepares chocolate in the traditional manner, pouring it from a great height to create a froth. Chocolate has retained its links with rituals and religion.

top-selling boxes of assorted chocolates, of which there are now numerous varieties, including Cadbury's Roses, introduced in 1938. In 1935 the Aero bar, with its bubble-filled centre, was launched. 'Have you ever felt the bubbles melt?' asks the wrapper. Plain and mint varieties are now available. Maltesers, chocolate-covered balls with a Horlicks-flavoured centre, were originally marketed in 1936 as 'Energy Balls'.

The KitKat, made from chocolate-coated fingers of crisp, praline-filled wafer, appeared in 1936, and was first launched as Rowntree's Chocolate Crisp. It was not given the name KitKat until after the Second World War. The name comes from the Kit Kat Club, a low-ceilinged literary club in London where the oblong pictures (known colloquially as as 'kit-kats') on its walls were a feature. There are now ten factories worldwide producing KitKat, their output amounting to over 13 billion fingers a year. The familiar red and white wrapper was introduced in 1973. In 1999 the new KitKat Chunky, a single large bar, appeared. Rowntree's Smarties, dating from 1936, are sold in their distinctive tube, and the Nestlé Rowntree Smarties Easter egg is Nestlé's best-selling Easter egg. After Eights, the 'after-dinner mint', created a whole new market in 1963, although the manufacturer, Nestlé, claims that one in ten people buy After Eights to eat themselves, rather than to share or to give as a present. Today, up to six million individual After Eights are produced every day, and they are sold in 60 countries worldwide. Terry's Chocolate Orange represented an innovation in style, with its distinctive concept. Hershey's Kisses were launched in America in 1907.

QUIN

PHOSP

QUINQUINA
PHOSPHATE
DE LA
GRANDE
TRAPPE

EMMOULAGE ET

CHOC

GANACHE REVIVES FRENCH CREATIVITY

Realising that chocolate singular had now evolved into chocolates plural, France quickly seized the opportunity that this new market offered. For Robert Linxe, 'the chocolatier's skill lies in finding the perfect recipe'. His shop-cum-studio bears the name *La Maison du Chocolat*, and he has taken the art of ganache to new heights. He takes shavings of preferably plain couverture (a coating chocolate used in the confectionery trade), and adds them carefully to the simmering creamy liquid. The mixture then gently melts into a slick, glossy, thickened paste. The flavours of a perfect ganache should never drown the aroma of cocoa. Instead, whether they are creamy, caramel or fruity, they should enhance the bouquet. 'The essence of a well-made chocolate should only become apparent in stages, as it dissolves in the mouth.' Invigorating at the beginning, soothing in the middle and long lasting at the end: French craftsmen follow the rule faithfully. To maintain individuality of taste, some are now beginning to make their own couverture chocolate.

MONASTERIES

The nutritional value of chocolate helped monks to endure long periods of fasting. They assumed the right to make it themselves.

'It's a chocolatier's trademark, his handle,' Stéphane Bonnat of Maison Bonnat in Voiron (Isère) explains. Designer chocolatiers select cocoa beans of different origins to create complex blends, or they roast cocoa beans of the same origin in their quest for a pure taste. Competition for the small craftsman arived in the shape of the company Valrhona of Tain-l'Hermitage. In 1984 they went into large-scale production of 'cru' chocolate (meaning from a single crop), with guarantees of high quality. They manufactured couverture chocolate for the professionals, and an enticing new range of chocolate for the public at large. Valrhona chocolate is internationally renowned for quality, and recommended by the Chocolate Society.

TEMPTATION IN THE GARDEN OF EDEN

Eating chocolate is still seen by some as sinful, and they compare indulging a sweet tooth with the apple that Adam and Eve simply couldn't resist. Of all foods it's the one that best conveys the notion of pleasure, representing both forbidden pleasure and total bliss. This myth, which has been shaped in peoples' minds throughout the centuries, has its roots in the beliefs that existed in 1519, when Hernan Cortés first stepped onto American soil. When the conquistadors discovered *xocoatl* they became drawn into its world of legend and excess. The king drank it daily, and great quantities were consumed by the higher Aztec officials at banquets. During religious services priests plastered it on their faces. They even drank cocoa that had been dyed deep red with annatto for ceremonial purposes. The scarlet colour represented human blood that, according to legend, was the blood of a princess, deified because she had been savagely sacrificed. The bitterness of the cocoa beans represented the suffering that she had endured. Ordinary people, however, had little or no access to the drink, but they believed in the sacred powers of fertility attributed to the seeds. So, before the seeds were were planted, men would sleep with their wives, supposedly rendered fertile by the rituals attached to the cocoa bean's cultivation. The Spanish were drawn into the aura of mystery and sensuality surrounding chocolate, adapting its properties to suit their own tastes, and revering it for its nourishing, stimulating, mildly aphrodisiac, if not actually magical, properties.

THE BLESSING OF THE POPE

The Spanish colonists became positively addicted to chocolate and started to drink it every day. A series of rituals was established, where chocolate accompanied the first meal of the day at eight o'clock in the morning, or, *à la chicolade*, as it was called. Out travelling they would stop at the many *chocolaterias* along the busiest routes. Fresh chocolate was available all day long and was even served in churches. According to the story told by the Dominican monk Thomas Gage, women in the town of Chiapa would pretend to be suffering from stomach pains if, during 'low mass and even more so during high mass and the sermon', they were not able to partake of hot chocolate and some preserves. Although the bishops were also great fans of the chocolate drink, they would have preferred more spiritual worship, and it annoyed them to see their churches turned into restaurants. After many a strong

CHOCOLATE, THE PANACEA

As this van Houten advertisement suggests, chocolate isn't just a treat, it is also an excellent tonic for children, the sick, and young mothers.

warning they finally forbade the consumption of food and drink during divine worship, but there was an outcry. The Spanish ladies continued to take their chocolate during Mass, protected by the drawn swords of their husbands. Blood flowed, and the parishioners decided to attend services in convents instead where there was a greater degree of tolerance and where monks and nuns were constantly seeking the perfect chocolate recipe.

From the outset, the Church had authorised the consumption of chocolate during periods of fasting. However, taking the view that indulging the senses could not be anything other than bad for the soul, some of the clergy suggested to Pope Pius V that perhaps chocolate should be regarded as a food and as such be forbidden during periods of abstinence. They feared that the nutritional riches of this product would wipe out all the benefits of abstinence during a fast. Against all expectations, the Pope showed clemency, announcing that chocolate was indeed a drink and should therefore still be allowed. After his death the clergy made further attempts to have it excluded from religious services, but finally chocolate was officially permitted by the Church in the 18th century. It was decreed that, like wine, it did not break the fast.

CACAO VAN HOUTEN.
Meilleur que tous les chocolats.

DOCTORS DECIDE THAT CHOCOLATE IS GOOD FOR YOU

Chocolate began its conquest of the aristocracy of Europe, who monopolised it, maintaining that it was a luxury item beyond the reach of the ordinary people. But a new debate began to worry them. Scientists had not yet reached agreement on the beneficial effects of chocolate on health. And should it be drunk hot or should one rather have it cold? Did it really cure stomach pain? Was it really a stimulant? Opinion was divided, and there were claims and counter-claims. The physician and chocolate-manufacturer Sir Hans Sloane was firmly in favour, and marketed his drinking chocolate as an aid to digestion as a result of his findings in Jamaica, where 'Chocolate is here us'd by all People, at all times. The common use of this ... proves sufficiently its being a wholesome Food. The drinking of it actually warm, may make it the more Stomachic ...'. In her letters to her daughter, Madame de Grignan, the Marquise de Sévigné waxed and waned in praise of chocolate according to whim and fashion. Her recommendation on 11 February 1671 read: 'You do not feel well? You have not slept? Chocolate will restore you to health.' Some months later it was a completely different story: 'Chocolate is no longer for me what it was, fashion has led me astray, as it always does. All those who used to speak well of it now speak ill of it; they curse it, blaming it for all their ailments; it is the source of vapours and palpitations; it flatters you for a while, and then suddenly lights a continuous fever in you that leads to death ... In the name of God, don't keep it up.' Madame de Grignan, who was pregnant, did not pay much attention. She drank chocolate to ease her condition. Madame de Sévigné, somewhat reassured by her daughter's views, was again tempted : 'I wished to make my peace with chocolate; I took some chocolate night before last to digest my dinner, in order to have a good supper. I had some yesterday as sustenance so that I could fast until the evening. It had all the desired effects. What I find most pleasant about chocolate is that it acts according to one's wishes.' Shortly after birth, Madame de Grignan's daughter had a fever. The Marchioness thought she detected the ill effects of chocolate; a claim quickly forgotten since on 15 January 1672 she again advised her daughter to drink some chocolate in order 'that the most disagreeable company seems good'.

After some research, the medical profession finally decided that chocolate could help in the fight against anaemia. From that moment, in addition to seeking improvements to the production process, manufacturers like Cadbury in Britain and Menier and Poulain in France, strove to increase the accessibility of the 'food of the gods' to the common man. Now perceived as something that was good for you, chocolate was destined to become a

MID-AFTERNOON SNACK

Chocolate was seen as a healthy option for children, an energy-giving food useful as a mid-afternoon snack.

nutritional supplement for the general population, especially manual workers and children. Cadbury also aimed their cocoa advertising at athletes, captioning one of their posters with the words, 'Sustains against fatigue. Increases muscular strength. Gives physical endurance and staying power.'

A TORCH, A PENKNIFE, LASHINGS OF GINGER BEER AND ... CHOCOLATE

Rich in minerals (magnesium, potassium, phosphorus), milk chocolate is a source of calcium, necessary for a child's growth. In children's novels of the 1950s, children preparing to set off on an adventure would always be armed with a torch, a penknife and some chocolate for energy. And, after all, Milky Way was the sweet you could eat between meals, as the slogan proclaimed. However, with increasing prosperity in the West came a general diversification in food and lessening of physical activity. People ate better food and more calories, but took less exercise. By the 1960s and 1970s chocolate had well and truly become a victim of the diet-conscious society, obsessed with attaining the slimmest of figures that they saw paraded in the media every day. Children should not take chocolate to school with them, but rather a healthy apple or orange. No more eating chocolate on the grounds that it was good for your health, it would only pile on the pounds. This was

THE CACAO TREE
The cacao grows in the tropical forest in the shade of larger trees. Its fruits, or pods, grow straight out of the trunk and main branches and total on average 35 per year.

very depressing news for chocolate-lovers who went to ground, guiltily consuming their supplies in secret, away from the gaze of those who could resist or simply preferred savoury tastes. However, the medical profession has done some more research and decided that in fact chocolate is not harmful in moderation, and may even be good for you. Interviewed by the National Union of French Chocolatiers in January 1999, Doctor Didier Chapelot, a researcher in the physiology of alimentary behaviour in Paris, declared: 'Contrary to popular belief, a low-calorie diet with no chocolate does not make good sense. It's because of the pleasure factor. When an body is maintained in a state deficient in calories, as with most diets, the brain attributes a greater value to the foods most able to compensate for this deficit in energy. This added value manifests itself in an increase of perceived pleasure. Self-restraint leads to a preference for the foods highest in calories, notably of lipidic origin. It is possible that abstaining from chocolate is not a withdrawal of pleasure ... but a withdrawal of desire. Suppressing chocolate in our diet perhaps amounts to preventing us from being creatures capable of feeling desire.' No restraint necessary then, unless the chocolate-lover wishes to turn him or herself into a dry creature of abstinence, which by very definition is an unlikely state of affairs.

CHOCOLATE AS AN APHRODISIAC

The first chocolate of the day or just the smell of a freshly unwrapped chocolate bar is nectar to the sweet-toothed, just as much as the first chocolate that was served to the ladies of the 17th-century courts. It is said that a good many of them drank a cup of chocolate every two hours. Perhaps they were trying to gratify their sexual pleasures, just like King Montezuma, who drank chocolate daily in order, among other things, to honour his many wives. Did Casanova drink a cup every morning to help him on his amorous adventures? It is said that the cold Madame de Pompadour, mistress of Louis XV, drank chocolate to try to awaken her sexual feelings, while the unrestrained Madame du Barry, another of Louis' mistresses, confessed to drinking it in order to increase her already insatiable appetite. The supposed aphrodisiac properties of chocolate have been acknowledged for some time. Paradoxically, the Church, which permitted chocolate during times of fasting, disapproved in other circumstances, maintaining that an excessive consumption would lead inexorably to sins of the flesh. From a medical point of view, theobromine, which is found in chocolate, acts as a stimulant. John Gage, a Dominican friar, kept himself awake by drinking chocolate twice a day, in the morning and at the start of the evening, and Napoleon drank it before a battle. Since the 1970s chocolate has been known to have an antidepressant effect brought about by the action of two chemical ingredients, salsolinol (an alkaloid) and phenylethylamine (a stimulant related to amphetamines). Chocolate promotes such feelings of well-being, enjoyment and calm that some people become 'addicts' and need a regular 'fix' of their particular drug. Recently, neurologists have found that chocolate contains anandamide, a neurotransmitter whose effects are similar to those of cannabis, heightening sensations and euphoria.

FROM THE BEAN TO THE BAR
Whether in the form of cocoa powder, plain or milk block chocolate, or confectionery, the quality of chocolate depends on the choice of cocoa bean.

SO, IS CHOCOLATE GOOD FOR YOU?

These scientific investigations could explain the obsession with chocolate sometimes observed in heavy 'users' or the real 'chocoholics'. The symptoms of dependency are heightened physical and mental activity causing an individual to seek strong sensory stimulation for immediate pleasure. Eating or drinking chocolate is closely linked to pleasure, the satisfying of the senses and hedonistic values. However, other research points to the conclusion that the stimulant and anandamide content of chocolate is too low to cause addiction, and the 'hit' so desired by chocolate addicts is more a factor of the high sugar content. The Biscuit, Cake, Chocolate and Confectionery Alliance have calculated that it would take about 4,000 bars of milk chocolate to produce an aphrodisiac effect. However, chocolate may, indeed, be good for you. In fact, bizarrely, it may be good for your teeth. Japanese researchers have concluded that chocolate has anti-bacterial properties, which attack the Streptococcus bacteria responsible for tooth decay. Recent research has also concentrated on the polyphenols found in chocolate. Polyphenols are antioxidants, which help prevent blocked arteries by reducing the oxidation of cholesterol in the blood. The effect of eating a chocolate bar peaks after two hours, and continues for a total of 10 hours. Harvard University has produced research concluding that regular eaters of chocolate (and other candy) actually live a little longer than those who abstain. The researchers surmise that the polyphenol content is responsible. Chocolate is also a useful source of vitamins, and according to another study an average bar provides 21 per cent of the RDA (recommended daily amount) of calcium and 12 per cent of iron. Amazingly, they also report that the mere smell of chocolate boosts the immune system by producing a powerful antibody.

CLUBS AND EXHIBITIONS

To satisfy the demands of chocolate consumers and promote the industry, clubs and societies devoted to chocolate have opened up all over the world. In Britain there are two: The Chocolate Society and The Chocolate Club.

CHOCOLATE TODAY

A new market has recently opened up in Japan. The Japanese palate is unused to sweet-tasting foods and prefers bitter chocolate with a high cocoa content. The Chinese have yet to develop a taste for chocolate, but the market there is potentially immense.

It is a long time since the Aztec 'food of the gods' first made its way to the shores of Western Europe. Since then chocolate has had its ups and downs, being associated with gluttony and health-giving properties in turn. However, one thing is for sure, regardless of whether it has been in or out of favour officially, it has always been enjoyed by the consumer and will continue to do so for many years to come.

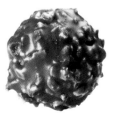

LOOK

DURING THE 19TH CENTURY CHOCOLATE BECAME MORE WIDELY AVAILABLE.
POSTERS ADVERTISING CHOCOLATE PRODUCTS SPREAD THE GOOD NEWS
AND REMINDED PEOPLE AS THEY WENT ABOUT THEIR DAILY LIVES THAT
WHAT THEY NEEDED WAS A LITTLE CHOCOLATE.
THESE OLD POSTERS FROM AROUND THE WORLD MAKE
A NOSTALGIC COLLECTION TODAY.

'Some confectioners buy their supplies already tempered, but I like to do it myself.'

There is an endless fascination in handling the raw dullish blocks of couverture,

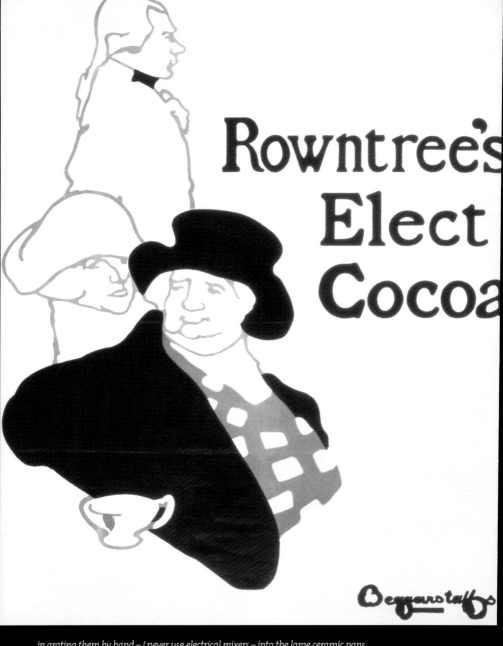

Rowntree's
Elect
Cocoa

Beggarstaffs

in grating them by hand – I never use electrical mixers – into the large ceramic pans,

then melting, stirring, testing each painstaking step

CHOCOLAT DE L'UNION

LYON

... just the right amount of heat has been applied to make the change.

There is a kind of alchemy in the transformation of base chocolate

into this wise fool's gold, a layman's magic, which even my mother might have relished.

As I work I clear my mind, breathing deeply.

MAKERS TO
H.M. THE KING, H.M. THE QUEEN

BY APPOINTMENT
H.M. QUEEN ALEXANDRA

FRY'S
PURE
BREAKFAST
COCOA

MANUFACTURED BY

J.S. FRY & SONS, L?

BRISTOL & LONDON

Raised on It!

the copper pans, the rising vapour from the melting couverture.

The mingled scents of chocolate, vanilla, heated copper and cinnamon are intoxicating,

powerfully suggestive; the raw and earthy tang of the Americas,

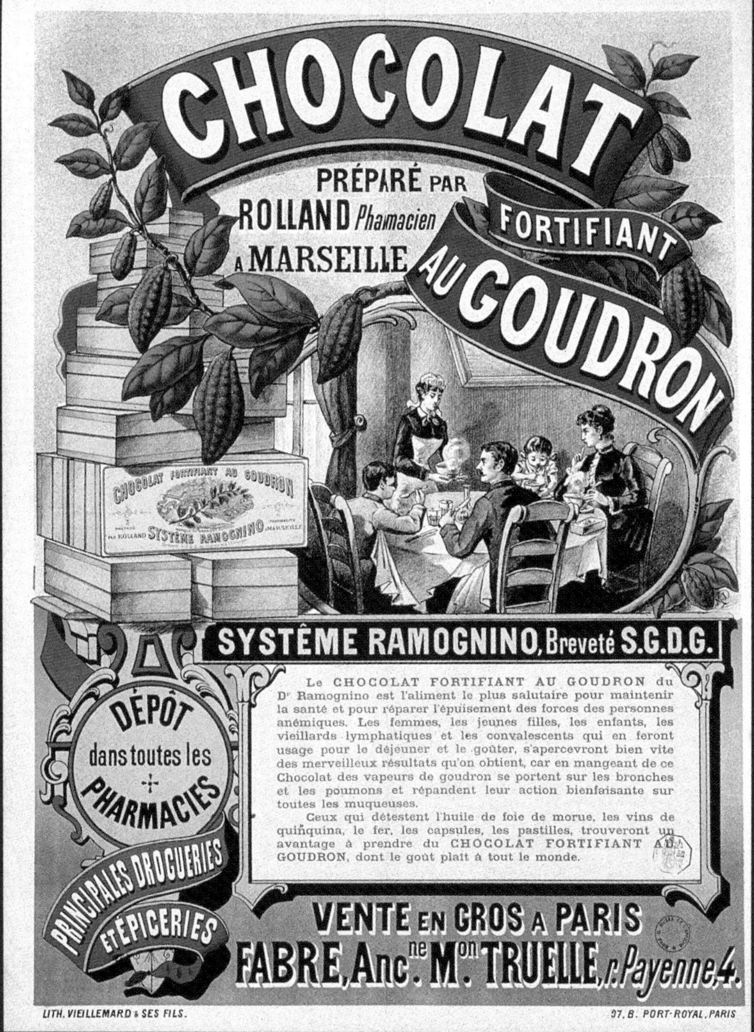
CHOCOLAT
PRÉPARÉ PAR
ROLLAND Phamacien
A MARSEILLE
FORTIFIANT
AU GOUDRON
CHOCOLAT FORTIFIANT AU GOUDRON
PRÉPARÉ PAR ROLLAND SYSTÈME RAMOGNINO PHARMACIEN A MARSEILLE
SYSTÈME RAMOGNINO, Breveté S.G.D.G.
Le CHOCOLAT FORTIFIANT AU GOUDRON du Dr Ramognino est l'aliment le plus salutaire pour maintenir la santé et pour réparer l'épuisement des forces des personnes anémiques. Les femmes, les jeunes filles, les enfants, les vieillards lymphatiques et les convalescents qui en feront usage pour le déjeuner et le goûter, s'apercevront bien vite des merveilleux résultats qu'on obtient, car en mangeant de ce Chocolat des vapeurs de goudron se portent sur les bronches et les poumons et répandent leur action bienfaisante sur toutes les muqueuses.
Ceux qui détestent l'huile de foie de morue, les vins de quiñquina, le fer, les capsules, les pastilles, trouveront un avantage à prendre du CHOCOLAT FORTIFIANT AU GOUDRON, dont le goût plait à tout le monde.
DÉPÔT dans toutes les PHARMACIES
PRINCIPALES DROGUERIES ET ÉPICERIES
VENTE EN GROS A PARIS
FABRE, Ancne Mon TRUELLE, r. Payenne, 4.
LITH. VIEILLEMARD & SES FILS.
97, B. PORT-ROYAL, PARIS

A seat in the sun, the scent of flowers,—

and everything in the garden is lovely!

Lovelier still if you have Quality Street — a wonderful assortment

of eighteen deliciously different chocolates and toffees.

Mackintosh's
'Quality Street'
REG^D

Eighteen delicious varieties of chocolates and toffees

PAS de voyage
SANS
CHOCOLAT

The bitter elixir of life.' Extract from Chocolat *by Joanne Harris, Doubleday, 1999.*

IN PRACTICE

CHOCOLATE PLAYS AN IMPORTANT ROLE IN THE ECONOMY OF
MANY OF THE WORLD'S TROPICAL COUNTRIES.
HOW DOES IT FIND ITS WAY TO THE EUROPEAN MANUFACTURERS?
WHICH COUNTRY CONSUMES THE MOST AND DO NATIONAL TASTES VARY?
DELICIOUS CHOCOLATE RECIPES FOR TOTAL INDULGENCE.

Cocoa-producing countries

Cacao trees grow on 5 million hectares (12.3 million acres) of land along the equator. Eight countries account for more than 80 per cent of world cocoa production. The revenue derived from cocoa plays a major part in the survival of small plantations.

Maximum production from small operations

Cocoa production (the fermenting and drying of cocoa beans) has climbed to third place in the world league of food commodities, after sugar and coffee. In Latin America, Africa, and South East Asia, 45 countries owe either all or a significant proportion of their economies to cocoa production. Eight of them account for 80 per cent of total production, estimated in 1997 at 2.6 million tonnes. The cocoa trade has a turnover of £1.65 billion. The producing countries, usually part of the developing world, rely on this indispensable source of income for the survival of their plantations. They are frequently fairly modest in size, covering an area of less than 10 hectares (25 acres) and belong for the most part to small farming families.

TRINIDAD
1,200 tonnes
The trinitario, a hybrid that produces a cocoa high in fat, was developed here.

ECUADOR
70,000 tonnes
Farms of around 5 hectares (12 acres), some of which concentrate on growing 'nacional' cocoa with the distinctive jasmine aroma, known as 'arriba'.

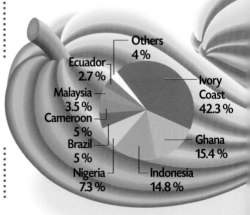

Others 4%
Ecuador 2.7%
Malaysia 3.5%
Cameroon 5%
Brazil 5%
Nigeria 7.3%
Ivory Coast 42.3%
Ghana 15.4%
Indonesia 14.8%

NATIONAL PRODUCTION FIGURES FOR 1997-8 (SOURCE: CIRAD, CENTRE FOR INTERNATIONAL COOPERATION AND AGRICULTURAL RESEARCH).

66

IVORY COAST
1,100,000 tonnes
Top producer, with a 40 per cent share of the market, the Ivory Coast produces standard cocoas with a robust flavour. It supplies a large proportion of the major manufacturers.

NIGERIA
190,000 tonnes
The failure to replant ageing plantations has led to a fall in production.

VENEZUELA
150,000 tonnes
Some of the finest cocoas in the world are grown here, among them the chuao variety. It is prized for its elegance and strong, hot flavour.

GHANA
400,000 tonnes
The advanced age of some plantations has pushed this country from first to second place in the rankings. The establishment of new plantations will allow revitalisation and increased production.

CAMEROON
130,000 tonnes
Cocoa is Cameroon's principal export, but it has suffered badly from black pod disease, and recently half the harvest has been destroyed.

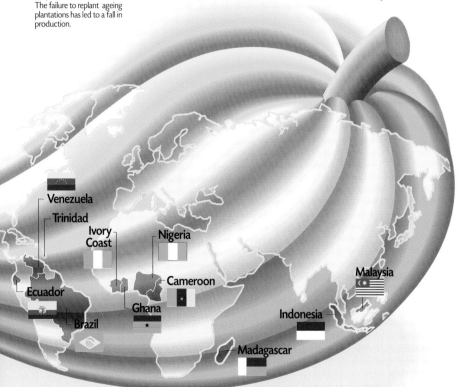

BRAZIL
130,000 tonnes
Witch's broom disease has wiped out a large number of plantations. Brazil has fallen from second to seventh in world production.

MADAGASCAR
2,500 tonnes
High-quality criollo varieties grow on small plantations.

INDONESIA
385,000 tonnes
Cacao trees are cultivated intensively both by the state and by private owners. Apart from some Java cocoa varieties, the others are of only average quality.

MALAYSIA
90,000 tonnes
Malaysia boasts some important cocoa processing operations. Unfortunately, its cocoa is of a fairly poor quality.

The cacao tree

Originally grown in central America, the cacao tree was introduced into Africa at the end of the 19th century but did not reach Indonesia and Malaysia until the 1970s.

In the shade of the tropics

The cacao tree, *Theobroma cacao*, which in Greek means 'food of the gods', thrives in the hot, humid climate of tropical forests. It grows up to an altitude of 700 metres (2,300 ft), often at the foot of larger trees, which offer protection from the sun with their higher branches. Its tap-root descends deep into the soil. Above ground it can reach a height of 12 metres (40 ft) in the wild, but when cultivated it is kept to a height of 6 metres (20 ft).Its fragile bark is silvery-grey in colour and its evergreen leaves are normally about 30 cm (1 ft) long, and provide welcome shade for the farmers working beneath. Unusually, the buds, flowers and fruits grow straight out of the trunk and main branches. The botanical term for this very rare characteristic is cauliflory. The cacao tree first flowers when it is three years old and matures at six years. The flower buds burst into 'flower cushions' of thousands of tiny, delicate, scentless flowers, which may be white, pink, yellow or red depending on the variety. Only those that have been fertilised either by insects or manually by the farmers (about 1 per cent) turn into fruits or pods.

Types of cacao tree

Three main classifications of cacao tree are grown in the plantations. The criollo, nicknamed the 'Caracas', is the original tree and grows only at high altitude in regions of high rainfall. Its beans produce a fine, richly aromatic, much prized cocoa (scarcely 5 per cent of global production). The best crops come from the islands of Trinidad and Jamaica and also from Venezuela and Grenada. The forestero, or 'foreigner', makes up 80 per cent of world cocoa production. This vigorous variety, which originated in the Amazon region, now grows principally in Africa. Because it is bitter and acidic, it is used in the manufacture of mass-market chocolate products. The trinitario is a cross between the other two varieties, and was developed in Trinidad, although it is also grown in Venezuela and Sri Lanka. High in fat and with a strong aroma, it is the basis of fine cocoas with subtle flavours.

The pods

A cacao tree produces between 20 and 80 pods a year, the average being around 35. Shaped rather like rugby balls, they are 20 cm (8 in) long and at most 15 cm (6 in) wide, and orange-brown in colour. The pods mature after four to six months, when they weigh around 380 g (13 oz). Inside, a layer of sweet, acidic pulp, called mucilage, protects around 40 seeds. Rather like haricot beans, 55 per cent of the mass of cocoa beans is taken up by two cotyledons, which give them a high fat content. In addition, the beans contain polyphenols (a group of chemicals that include antioxidants) and tannins (7 per cent), caffeine (0.2 per cent), theobromine, a stimulant (2 per cent), carbohydrates (12 per cent), proteins (10 per cent), fibre (17 per cent), mineral salts and trace elements (2 per cent).

A cocoa plantation

In response to the growth in consumption, producers have to contend with the problems of ageing plantations and greater market competition. One solution is better management of the farms by tackling disease and developing cocoa of a higher quality.

An emphasis on quality

Disorganised plantation management and greater market competition threaten the future of cocoa production. Up to 90 per cent of commercial chocolate products are made from the common cocoa varieties, but the quality needs to be improved, whichever type of cocoa is produced, whether high grade or destined for the mass market. Trees that have a high yield yet produce less fragrant cocoa are being replaced by more suitable plants. The development of higher quality cocoa will increase demand for '100 per cent pure' chocolate, or organic chocolate, thereby bringing about increased productivity, the establishment of co-operatives and a better standard of living for the farmer.

Forest cover after thinning and partial burning

1.5–2 metres (5–6 ft) rainfall; dry season less than three months

Altitude lower than 600 m (2,000 ft)

Can be combined, for example, with banana trees

It is estimated that disease destroys 40 per cent of world cocoa production each year. Black pod disease is rife in Africa, where the offending fungus, *Phytophthora*, infects the surface of the cacao pod with a brown spot, which gradually penetrates the pod and destroys its contents. Chemical control is much too difficult for small farmers. Witch's broom, found in South America, suffocates the 'flower cushions' and vegetative buds on the cacao tree. The tree stops producing fruit, and many spindly branches develop, like a witch's broom. To stop the spread of the disease the infected parts have to be removed twice a year.

Equatorial region: temperature never below 15°C (59°F), no strong, drying winds

After three years the first cocoa beans are harvested. Some 30 years later, the cacao trees have almost stopped producing and are abandoned in favour of newer plantations.

Light, deep soil, rich in minerals and organic matter

Cocoa beans

Methods for cultivating and harvesting the beans have remained the same since the first plantations were established. All operations, from harvesting to fermenting the beans, are still carried out manually, so the industry at grass roots level is very labour intensive.

The pods are fragile, so they have to be picked with care. To prevent germination of the seeds inside the pods, they are split open as soon as they are harvested. Protected by mucilage, the cacao seeds are removed and fermentation begins. It takes two days for the finer cocoa seeds to ferment and transform into beans, and seven days for the remainder. Before they are put into sacks ready to be exported, some of their moisture has to be removed. They are left in the sun for one to two weeks, and are turned periodically. It is at this point that their quality is assessed. The best quality beans are brown in the centre. Reclassified as fine cocoa, these form the basis for the best chocolate. The other beans, brownish-purple in colour, are classified as standard cocoa. There is also a third category just at the limit of commercial acceptability that, naturally, commands only very low prices.

1 The pods growing lower down the tree are cut with secateurs; higher up, a long knife or pruning hook must be used.

The subtlety of cocoa blends

Cocoa is the result of blending several varieties of cocoa bean together, the dominant ones being criollo, forestero and trinitario. Reference is also made to the beans' provenance, and occasionally the domaine or particular plantation is specified. Cocoa from Madagascar is strong and slightly acrid. Sri Lankan and Indonesian cocoas are very scented and have a spicy aftertaste, while Caribbean cocoa has an enticing, well-balanced flavour with notes of dried fruits. The arriba from Ecuador has a very floral aroma, with notes of jasmine. The most acidic cocoa of all comes from Sumatra, and the most full-bodied from the Ivory Coast. The hot and fruity *gran couva* originates from a single Trinidadian plantation. The Hacienda Concepción in Venezuela produces a fragrant cocoa.

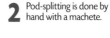

2 Pod-splitting is done by hand with a machete.

3 The cocoa beans are placed on banana leaves or into wooden boxes where fermentation begins. The seeds stop their germination process. Starting out a whitish colour, they turn to a mahogany brown. At the same time their aroma develops.

4 The growers dry the beans on mats on the ground or on drying tables, the moisture content falling from 60 to 7 per cent.

From cocoa to chocolate

Cocoa is processed to produce not only cocoa butter and cocoa powder but also couverture chocolate, used by specialist chocolate makers.

Raw cocoa beans arrive at the chocolate factory in jute sacks. They are cleaned to eliminate all extraneous matter and then roasted. As they lose moisture they acquire their chocolate colour and develop their aroma. Once cooled they are crushed into small pieces or 'nibs'. A hydraulic press then transforms the cocoa into cocoa mass, by heating and compressing the ground cocoa nibs, allowing the fat, or cocoa butter, to run off. When the compression chamber is opened the resulting cakes are released and then pulverised into raw cocoa powder, ready for 'dutching', or alkalising.

Couverture chocolate

To make couverture chocolate, which is the essential ingredient in luxury chocolate confectionery, cocoa butter and sugar are added to cocoa mass. The mixture is kneaded and then ground to reduce the size of the granules in the cocoa mass. In order to develop the chocolate aroma and make the chocolate into a smooth liquid, the cocoa mass undergoes a process called conching. The conches agitate up to a tonne of chocolate.

Before it takes on its final form (either liquid or block), the chocolate undergoes a process called tempering, during which its temperature is gradually lowered from 50°C (122°F) until the desired consistency is achieved.

COCOA BEANS

Cleaning and crushing

ROASTING
10–30 minutes. Standard cocoa is roasted at a temperature of 120–130°C (248–266°F); fine cocoa below 120°C (248°F).

Grinding and refining

COCOA MASS
(or cocoa liquor)

THE DIFFERENT FORMS OF CHOCOLATE

ASSORTED CHOCOLATES
Assorted chocolates are individual chocolates or ones with different shapes, consisting of a variety of fillings encased in a quality couverture. The varieties of filling are legion: caramel, pralines (giandujas), liqueurs, nougats, truffles, ganaches and fruit-flavoured creams.

BLOCK CHOCOLATE
Plain
Cocoa butter, cocoa (less than 50 per cent for mass-market products, or more than 50 per cent for bitter and extra-bitter, '100 per cent pure', 'cru', and organic varieties) and sugar.
Milk
Cocoa, cocoa butter, milk and sugar.
White
Cocoa butter, sugar and milk.
Chocolate blended with other ingredients
Plain, milk or white chocolate to which have been added hazelnuts, crisped rice, honey, raisins or nougat, etc.

FILLED CHOCOLATE
Plain, milk or white chocolate, with a fruit or almond paste, or nougatine filling, etc.

CHOCOLATE BARS
Designed as a snack and for individual consumption. Contain dried fruits, cereals, caramel, biscuit, etc.

CHOCOLATE CONFECTIONERY
Handmade individual chocolates, nut clusters, pastilles, dragées and chocolate balls all fall under the general term of chocolate confectionery. Other ingredients can be added, such as caramel, crisped rice, peanuts, etc.

COCOA POWDER
Used to make hot drinks and in cooking. Varieties include pure cocoa powder, sweetened cocoa powder and blended cocoa powder (with added malt, milk or starch).

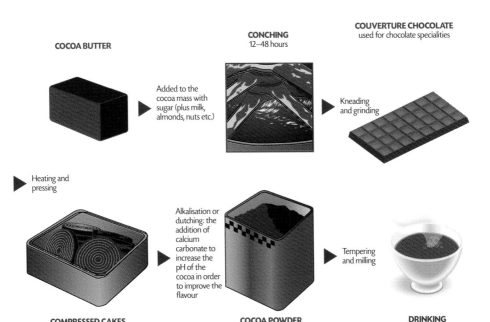

COCOA BUTTER

Added to the cocoa mass with sugar (plus milk, almonds, nuts etc.)

CONCHING
12–48 hours

Kneading and grinding

COUVERTURE CHOCOLATE
used for chocolate specialities

Heating and pressing

COMPRESSED CAKES

Alkalisation or dutching: the addition of calcium carbonate to increase the pH of the cocoa in order to improve the flavour

COCOA POWDER

Tempering and milling

DRINKING CHOCOLATE

The world chocolate market

The large chocolate manufacturing companies are head to head in a desperate struggle to increase their market share. They dream up more and more diverse products to appeal to a greater number of consumers.

No cocoa, no chocolate! Buyers representing dealers or manufacturers trawl the length and breadth of cocoa plantations, selecting the raw material and checking for quality. The buyers judge the potential of future cocoa harvests or beans already in stock on the spot, their comments influencing the price of a tonne of raw cocoa on the commodity markets of New York, London and Paris.

A clash of Titans

In a bid to maintain a demand in the market, some cocoa producers will not hesitate to burn part of their harvest. Others organise themselves into co-operatives to pool their resources and enable them to compete with the larger producers. Some estates even purchase their own cocoa-processing equipment. What are these initiatives really worth? Very little, when compared with the might of the independent processing companies in the West, which increase their power and presence by means of mergers or partnerships with dealers. Grace Cacao, part of the Archer Daniels Midland group, Barry-Callebaut and Cargill are the three largest cocoa pressing plants in the world.

These manufacturing companies make cocoa for specialist chocolate houses or for certain brand names. From the ground cocoa beans they produce not only cocoa mass, cocoa butter and cocoa powder, but also couverture chocolate, chocolate for filling and chocolate for glazing. In addition to these giant cocoa manufacturing companies, there are also large corporations in the food and agriculture industry which manufacture their own products and sell them in the mass market.

CHOCOLATE PRODUCTION IN INDUSTRIALISED COUNTRIES

SOURCE: INTERNATIONAL STATISTICS, 1998 OF CAOBISCO/ICCO (ASSOCIATION OF THE CHOCOLATE, BISCUIT AND CONFECTIONERY INDUSTRIES/INTERNATIONAL COCOA ORGANISATION). IN THOUSANDS OF TONNES.

UNITED STATES
1.48

GERMANY
0.89

GREAT BRITAIN
0.50

FRANCE
0.38

BRAZIL
0.33

THE SPECIALIST MARKET

Barry Callebaut processes 11 per cent of world production. With a 35 per cent stake in the market, the company is the number one supplier to the specialist chocolate trade. Resulting from a Swiss-French merger, the company is a subsidiary of Klaus J. Jacob. Annual turnover is around £0.9 billion. Through 19 strategically located plants, Barry-Callebaut controls 40 per cent of the European couverture chocolate market, estimated at 750,000 tonnes. In Latin America the company has signed a contract with the Mexican government to establish cocoa plantations and factories in partnership with Chadler, a Brazilian cocoa manufacturer.

SWITZERLAND, LINDT & SPRUNGLI:
Lindt, Ghirardelli, Caffarel

SWITZERLAND, NESTLÉ:
Nestlé, Kholer, Crunch, Kit Kat, Lion, Cailler, Quality Street, Smarties, After Eight, Nuts, Menier, Lanvin, Galak, Frigor

ENGLAND, CADBURY-SCHWEPPES:
Cadbury, Poulain

ITALY, FERRERO:
Ferrero Rocher, Mon Chéri, Nutella, Kinder, Rafaello

GERMANY:
Stollwerck

UNITED STATES:
Hershey's

UNITED STATES, MARS:
Mars, M&M's, Milky Way, Snickers, Twix, Bounty

UNITED STATES, KRAFT-JACOB-SUCHARD:
Suchard, Milka, Toblerone, Suchard, Daim, Côte d'Or

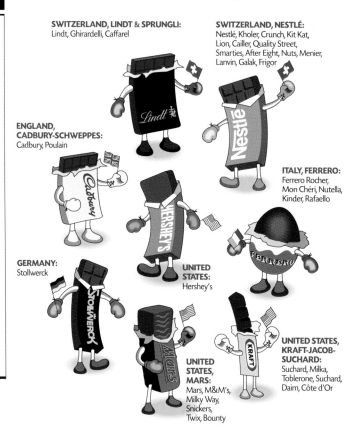

JAPAN 0.20   ITALY 0.20   HOLLAND 0.18   BELGIUM 0.16   SPAIN 0.13   AUSTRALIA 0.12   SWITZERLAND 0.11

Chocolate and the consumer

Chocolate consumption is rocketing: 79 per cent of all chocolate lovers are to be found in Europe and North America. Each country within these two sectors, however, has a different notion of just exactly what good chocolate is. However, one product does seem to be emerging as favourite: the humble chocolate bar.

The taste of the nation

In the United Kingdom we eat on average 3.15 kg (6.93 lb) of filled bars and block chocolate a year and 2.04 kg (4.49 lb) of solid block chocolate. In Europe the Danes, Norwegians and Swedes regard chocolate as a source of energy to fight against the cold. Between them they eat an average of 7.49 kg (16.48 lb) of chocolate per person per year. Compare that with the average consumption in hotter Mediterranean countries, such as Portugal, Greece and Spain, where consumption is only 3.94 kg (8.67 lb) per person per year. The Spanish have retained their liking for drinking chocolate from the days

of their conquest of the New World. Theirs is the only nation to use a significant amount of cocoa powder – 0.39 kg (0.86 lb) per person per year. The Germans and Italians are fond of chocolate spreads, such as bicerin (an Italian speciality), which often replaces sugar in coffee. Historically, the British and the Americans have preferred solid chocolate. They are the leading consumers of the much-loved chocolate bar, a product for which Spain has only recently developed a real liking, consumption rising from 0.01 kg (0.02 lb) in 1993 to 0.17 kg (0.37 lb) per person per year in 1998. Belgium, Ireland, Finland and France slowly but surely bring up the rear.

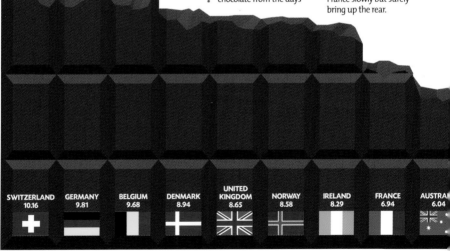

SWITZERLAND	GERMANY	BELGIUM	DENMARK	UNITED KINGDOM	NORWAY	IRELAND	FRANCE	AUSTRA
10.16	9.81	9.68	8.94	8.65	8.58	8.29	6.94	6.04

WORLD CONSUMPTION IN TYPES OF CHOCOLATE PRODUCT

AUSTRALIA
Assorted chocolates, chocolate confectionery: 1.81 kg (3.98 lb), sweets containing cocoa: 1.83 kg (4.03 lb).

BELGIUM
Filled bars and block chocolate: 3.52 kg (7.74 lb).

BRAZIL
Sweets containing cocoa: 1.25 kg (2.75 lb).

DENMARK
Assorted chocolates and other confectionery: 2.75 kg (6.05 kg), solid block chocolate: 2.57 kg (5.65 kg).

FINLAND
Assorted chocolates and other chocolate confectionery: 1.58 kg (3.48 kg), filled bars and block chocolate: 1.42 kg (3.12 kg).

FRANCE
Solid block chocolate: 1.93 kg (4.2 lb), assorted chocolates and other chocolate confectionery: 1.67 kg (3.67 lb).

GERMANY
Solid block chocolate: 1.50 kg (3.32 lb), chocolate spreads: 1.15 kg (2.53 lb).

IRELAND
White chocolate: 8.92 kg (19.62 lb), filled bars and block chocolate: 1.69 kg (3.72 lb).

ITALY
Assorted chocolates and other chocolate confectionery: 0.59 kg (1.30 lb), sweets containing cocoa: 0.76 kg (1.67 lb), chocolate spreads: 0.57 kg (1.25 lb).

JAPAN
Assorted chocolates and other chocolate confectionery: 0.68 kg (1.5 lb), chocolate sweets: 0.51 kg (1.12 lb).

PORTUGAL
Solid block chocolate: 0.44 kg (0.97 lb), filled bars and block chocolate 0.42 kg (0.92 lb), cocoa powder: 0.39 kg (0.86 lb).

SPAIN
Cocoa powder: 1.56 kg (3.43 lb), solid block chocolate: 0.85 kg (1.87 lb).

SWEDEN
Assorted chocolates and other chocolate confectionery: 2.43 kg (5.35 lb), solid block chocolate: 1.58 kg (3.47 lb).

SWITZERLAND
Solid block chocolate: 3.99 kg (8.78 lb), filled bars and block chocolate: 2.91 kg (6.40 lb).

UNITED KINGDOM
Filled bars and block chocolate: 3.15 kg (6.93 lb), solid block chocolate: 2.04 kg (4.49 lb).

UNITED STATES
Filled bars and block chocolate: 2.65 kg (5.83 lb).

SOURCE: INTERNATIONAL STATISTICS OF COCOA, CHOCOLATE AND SUGAR INDUSTRIES, 1998, IN KG PER PERSON PER YEAR WITH REFERENCE TO A SAMPLE OF SEVEN FAMILIES PER COUNTRY.

CONSUMPTION IN KGS PER PERSON PER COUNTRY IN 1998
SOURCE: INTERNATIONAL STATISTICS, 1998, OF CAOBISCO/ICCO (ASSOCIATION OF THE CHOCOLATE, BISCUIT AND CONFECTIONERY INDUSTRIES/INTERNATIONAL COCOA ORGANISATION).

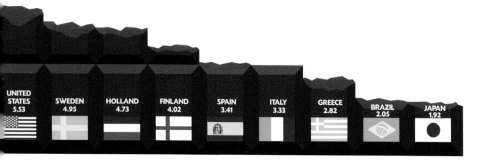

UNITED STATES	SWEDEN	HOLLAND	FINLAND	SPAIN	ITALY	GREECE	BRAZIL	JAPAN
5.53	4.95	4.73	4.02	3.41	3.33	2.82	2.05	1.92

European chocolate

European chocolates are generally made to include ingredients of the highest standard, and chocolatiers take a great pride in their work.

Origins and flavours

The specialist chocolate-makers, whose numbers have doubled in ten years, and the big manufacturers (Cadbury, Lindt, Nestlé, Valrhona) have all been working hard to perfect dark chocolate. The skill is in achieving the right balance of flavours. Dark chocolate is a tricky substance and can be compared with wine in its complexity. Subtelties of taste can be brought to the chocolate from the place where the cocoa beans were grown, echoing the importance of 'terroir' in wine production. French chocolate-makers have been making the most of this, developing very specific products, such as Valrhona's 'Grands Crus', Nestlé's 'Chocolats de terroirs', or Cliuzel's 'Chocolats d'hacienda' with names that are all meant to evoke the distinct characteristics of the cocoa's origins. Green and Black's Fairtrade Chocolate assures its high reputation for quality by using beans bought direct from the cocoa plantations.

Milk chocolate

The interest in milk chocolate in Britain is well established, with Cadbury's Dairy Milk representing the best-selling moulded chocolate bar. If it is well made, milk chocolate can provide an ideal complement to certain flavours by modifying their intensity with its sweetness and subtlety. But first all its imperfections, such as excessive greasiness and sweetness, which lingers in the mouth, have to be eliminated. Carefully chosen cocoa beans from carefully selected areas of origin, paired with vanilla and cream, have given rise to products such as Valrhona's Jivara, Nestlé's 'Lait arriba', and Côte d'Or's 'Noir de lait'.

Anything is possible

Chocolatiers are always on the look-out for new taste sensations and are ready to experiment with unusual textures and ingredients, adding essences of spices and herbs and fruit purées, or crunchy ingredients. Terry's Chocolate Orange combines chocolate and the tangy taste of orange in the unique segmented 'orange' design. Cadbury's produce a Creme Egg, full of white and yellow fondant. Lindt adds 'nibs' (fragments of cocoa bean) to its range of chocolate from Madagascar, Ecuador, and the Amazon. Suchard has a range of 'taster' milk chocolates combined with pieces of nougatine. In Paris, Gérard Mulot's Mélissa is a creamy liquorice ganache covered in dark chocolate.

HANDMADE CHOCOLATES
Robert Linxe, Maison du Chocolat.
Ganaches with dark rum, cinnamon and fennel, pralines with almond or caramel flavours, covered with milk chocolate.

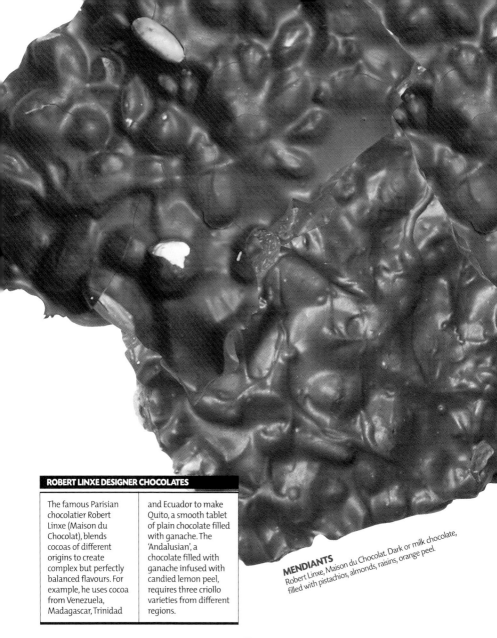

The famous Parisian chocolatier Robert Linxe (Maison du Chocolat), blends cocoas of different origins to create complex but perfectly balanced flavours. For example, he uses cocoa from Venezuela, Madagascar, Trinidad and Ecuador to make Quito, a smooth tablet of plain chocolate filled with ganache. The 'Andalusian', a chocolate filled with ganache infused with candied lemon peel, requires three criollo varieties from different regions.

MENDIANTS
Robert Linxe, Maison du Chocolat. Dark or milk chocolate, filled with pistachios, almonds, raisins, orange peel.

Italian chocolates – delicious little messages of love

Try a gianduja. Let it melt in your mouth, and it's gone before you know it. The gianduja expresses the Italian relationship with chocolate, both sensual and erotic.

Gianduja, goddess of Italian chocolate

Hazelnut, almond or milk chocolate? A perfect gianduja (unpronounceable to non-Italian speakers) induces a feeling of total bliss. This soft blend of hazelnuts, walnuts or almonds with milk chocolate wrapped in gold paper resembles a tiny gold ingot.

It was an Italian chocolate-maker called Gian D'la Duja who handed out this new creation to the crowds in Turin and gave it his name. Along with Baci (little kisses), each one containing a message, it has now become the epitome of the Italian chocolate. Nowadays, any confectioner in Piedmont worth his salt must include this type of chocolate in his repertoire. When the Fiat Tipo 4 was launched in

1911, chocolatier Manjani from Bologna created the cremino – which was renamed Fiat after the ceremony. This square of chocolate, almonds and hazelnuts in four different layers – two pale and two dark – remains a classic Italian speciality. It is a coffee-time tradition in some families in this region of northern Italy to serve a traditional paste called bicerin, made from cocoa, honey and hazelnuts, which replaces the sugar in their coffee.

GIANDUJA
This Italian speciality has become world famous: Godiva produces a gianduja wrapped in a traditional gold paper.

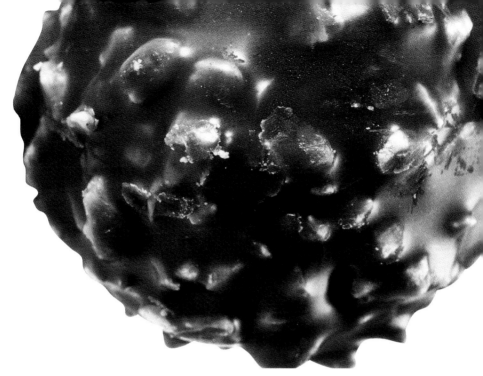

FERRERO ROCHER
These nut clusters have a wafer and soft hazelnut paste filling.

The delicious chocolate spread Nutella, so popular with children, is made by Ferrero. This Italian company, employing 6,000 people on four different production sites, developed their product from vegetable oils combined with hazelnuts, sugar, skimmed milk and only a minute amount of chocolate to avoid paying the prohibitive price of cocoa. Another top-selling Ferrero chocolate is Mon Chéri, but perhaps the most famous is the Ferrero Rocher, an ingenious combination of praline, nuts and wafer forming individual chocolates promoted as being the perfect coffee-time accompaniment to a sophisticated dinner party.

MON CHÉRI
Liqueur and cherry in a chocolate shell.

British chocolates – comfort and a very wide choice

Chocolate is a basic part of the British diet. The reason? Its sweetness and melt-in-the mouth qualities make it a major comfort food.

Very sweet chocolate

The British are extremely fond of chocolate and rank fifth in world consumption tables, consuming 8.65 kg (19 lb) per person per year. They remain faithful to the tried and tested products from the major manufacturers, many of which have been around for decades, such as KitKat and Milky Way. Milk chocolate is their favourite, but there is a chocolate bar to suit all tastes, from Old Jamaica rum and raisin bar to the Wispa Mint bar. Manufacturers nowadays produce bars of old favourites with a variety of different flavoured fillings – for example, the mint Aero – for those who want to try something new. As anyone who travels abroad will tell you, in terms of the sheer range of chocolate bars and products on offer, the British sweet shop is hard to beat.

AFTER EIGHT
Nestlé. A very slim chocolate square filled with mint cream.

FINGERS
Cadbury. A crunchy biscuit covered in plain, milk or white chocolate.

SPECIALIST CHOCOLATES MAKE SLOW PROGRESS

The British are very faithful to the 'old favourites' of the chocolate world and combined with their taste for sweet milk chocolate, the demand for specialist 'designer' chocolates is not as great as in other countries. A few attempts have been made to establish a presence in the British market by Continental manufacturers in the larger towns, but the most successful of the specialist firms is undoubtedly Thorntons, a British firm that has introduced variety at reasonable prices, while remaining faithful to the sweet British palate.

Belgian chocolates – a reputation for sheer luxury

The Belgians are renowned for their chocolates, particularly those made with fresh cream. A box of Belgian chocolates is therefore best kept in the fridge.

Gift boxes

Remember the man in black who abseiled down a tall building to deliver a box of chocolates and vanished into the night, all because the lady loved Milk Tray? It was the Belgians who made it all possible. In 1912 Jean Neuhaus introduced a solid chocolate shell that was able to contain runny or soft centres. Realising that a selection of these new chocolates would make an ideal gift, his wife placed them in gift boxes and the box of chocolates was born. Among other Belgian luxuries are filled bars of chocolate introduced by Jean Galler of the Jacques chocolate house in the late 1930s. These miniature 70 g (2½ oz) blocks of chocolate are available in a range of different flavours. Belgians still enjoy chocolate in bars, a tradition that goes back to 1870, when Charles Neuhaus, Jean's father, launched the Côte d'Or brand. Immortalised by the elephant logo on the wrapper, it is a classic Belgian chocolate with a rich flavour.

THE MANON

The specialist chocolate makers try to find a balance between flavour and consistency. Each maker has his or her own recipe for pralines. The delicious Manon, as produced by such chocolate houses as Léonidas and Godiva is a classic Belgian creation made from whipped mocha-flavoured butter cream and crushed nuts enveloped in a sugar coating. It can be called a chocolate only by virtue of the cocoa butter that replaces sugar. The Belgians indulge in many other chocolates made from praline. They can be combined with vanilla cream fillings or subtle combinations of almonds and fruit – mandarin, pineapple, raspberry, and so on – the possibilities are many and varied.

PRESENTATION BOX
Godiva. The best present of all, a box of chocolates, in this case pralines in every possible flavour.

American chocolate –
the chocolate bar as champion

To European tastes most of the specialities produced in the United States seem overly sweet. Often filled with peanut butter or a sickly cream filling, many of the products lack the sophistication of European-made chocolates. Nor is there any great variety available, surprising in such a huge country with a wide ethnic background.

An unlikely combination

What could be more American than Mom's apple pie? Answer: Reese's Peanut Butter Cups. A perennial American favourite, these contain peanut butter centres with a hint of salt and are very rich. If you are trying them for the first time, you probably won't be able to tackle too many!

Godiva in America

Hershey is the top brand in the United States. It is manufactured mainly for the domestic market, which has remained faithful to the brand since the late 19th century. Seeking to launch mass-market products at unbeatable prices, Milton Hershey founded the Hershey Chocolate Company, and had a profound impact on American taste. His little milk chocolate Kisses are said to be the best-selling chocolates in the United States. After

Mars (the number two brand), Godiva also has a significant market share. Originally a Belgian company, but now part of the American Campbell Soup group, it was the first European concern to invest in the market across the Atlantic. It owes a large part of its success to its very sweet specialities, which are adapted for the American palate.

M&M'S
Chocolates that never melt in your hand, coated in a colourful crispy shell.

The top of the range

Ghirardelli of San Francisco (recently acquired by the Swiss company, Lindt & Sprungli) holds the position of top premium chocolate manufacturer. Influenced by large American restaurateurs who have often been trained in France, Ghirardelli is currently working on sophisticated new recipes. Couvertures of a higher cocoa content and therefore an intentionally lower sugar content are being used to make such wonderful creations as chocolate-orange truffles, bitter sweet chocolate with dried apricots and ginger, and chocolate bars filled with caramel and macadamia nuts. Delicious.

MARS
A chocolate bar filled with nougat and soft caramel. Just right for a quick snack.

THE CHOCOLATE BAR

The Americans are avid consumers of chocolate bars. They devour 2.65 kg (5.83 lb) per person per year, enough to make the fortunes of Forrest Mars and Milton Hershey, the chocolate bar pioneers. In the 1920s these two major producers (who claim credit for the invention) came up with the idea of making a type of chocolate that didn't melt, even in the heat of summer, that you could eat anywhere and at any time. In America at the end of the Second World War the chocolate bar became the symbol of the victorious American GIs. They were particularly envied by Europeans who had not seen chocolate at all throughout the lean war years.

Swiss chocolate – making the most of creamy milk from alpine cows

With cows in every meadow and an abundant supply of rich, creamy milk, there had to be a way to put it to good use. It was thanks to this fortuitous combination that the Swiss were able to invent milk chocolate.

Milk chocolate

Milk chocolate was first produced successfully in 1875 by the Swiss chocolate-maker Daniel Peter after eight years of experimentation. He used condensed milk instead of fresh milk so that the cocoa would not be affected by the acidity. Swiss milk chocolate has its own distinctive, very milky flavour. Historically, the great manufacturers such as Nestlé have sold their chocolate in large bars, very often with old-fashioned wrappers showing views over the Swiss lakes. One particular wrapper, however, has become famous the world over. Suchard has been packaging Milka chocolate in a mauve wrapper depicting a Swiss cow grazing peacefully in a field since 1900. Although it is now made in France, it is still a typically Swiss product.

TOBLERONE

The unmistakable triangular-shaped bar. From individual size to 4 kg (8.8 lb) block, there's a Toblerone for every appetite.

The Swiss develop their own praline

Every manufacturer has his own version of praline. Toblerone is a kind of cross between Italian gianduja and Spanish turrón. More than 100 tonnes of Toblerone leave the Suchard factory in Berne every day. This triangular bar, shaped like the Alps, has been a big hit since 1908. Developed by the Munz Family in 1874, the long bars contain a combination of nougat, honey and almond pieces and, of course, chocolate. Camille Bloch is famous for two other classic, unique soft praline products, Torino and Ragusa.

Three hot chocolates and one chocolate mousse

Introduced as a hot milky drink to Britain by Sir Hans Sloane, after his visit to Jamaica, hot chocolate is popular in many different countries. It is traditionally served at the end of a meal, as a warming drink before bedtime or at breakfast.

Ingredients for 6 cups:
• 250g (9 oz) grated plain chocolate (or 4 tablespoons unsweetened cocoa powder)
• 1 litre (1³/₄ pt) milk
• 1 tablespoon corn oil
• 4 tablespoons sugar
• 1 egg yolk
• 1 vanilla pod
• 1 cinnamon stick
• nutmeg
• 150 g (5 oz) peanuts

Mix the grated chocolate, sugar, corn oil, egg yolk and a little milk in a basin. In a pan, heat the remaining milk, split vanilla pod, cinnamon stick and pinch of nutmeg. Remove from the heat, pour the chocolate mixture into the milk and stir. Simmer until it thickens, stirring continuously. Before serving, remove the vanilla pod and add 150g (5 oz) roasted peanuts (or almonds).

Reminiscent of the Mayan way of making chocolate, this is your chance to sip the drink of the gods!

Melt the chocolate in the boiling water. Add the boiling milk, sugar, and hot coffee. Beat vigorously until all ingredients are well blended. Serve immediately.

Ingredients for 6 cups:
• 250g (9 oz) plain chocolate (or 4 tablespoons unsweetened cocoa powder)
• 1 litre (1³/₄ pt) boiling milk
• 500 ml (18 fl oz) boiling water
• 125 cm (4 fl oz) strong coffee
• 200g (7 oz) sugar

**RECIPE
ROLLET PRADIER**

VIENNESE CHOCOLATE

On a visit to Naples an intellectual, Johann Volckammer, is said to have tasted a cup of chocolate. He took the cocoa beans back to Nuremberg in Germany from where they evenually crossed the frontier to Vienna.

In a bain-marie, melt the plain chocolate in the milk with the vanilla and cinnamon. Let it cool slightly. Add the egg yolks. Thicken over a low heat, stirring continuously. As soon as the mixture begins to boil take it off the heat. Before serving, add 1 teaspoon whipped cream to each cup.

Ingredients for 6 cups:
- *250g (9 oz) plain chocolate (or 4 tablespoons unsweetened cocoa powder)*
- *1 litre (1¾ pt) milk*
- *vanilla, cinnamon*
- *4 egg yolks*
- *whipped cream*

CHOCOLATE MOUSSE

Melt the chocolate in a large bowl, over hot water. Separate the eggs. Whisk the egg whites with the sugar until stiff. Add the 10 egg yolks and the double cream to the hot melted chocolate. Mix well, then gradually fold in the egg whites carefully, so that the mousse remains fluffy. Pour into ramekins or a large serving bowl, and refrigerate for 2 to 3 hours before serving.

Ingredients for 8 servings:
- *250 g (9 oz) double cream*
- *600 g (1 lb 5 oz) 70 per cent cocoa cooking chocolate*
- *10 eggs*
- *150 g (5 oz) sugar*

Chocolate Charlotte

Everyone loves chocolate charlotte, children and adults alike. Light and frothy, it can be made entirely of chocolate or be combined with morello cherries or candied peel. A simply delicious dessert.

Ingredients for the finger biscuits
- 50 g (2 oz) egg yolk
- 150 g (5 oz) sugar
- 40 g (1 ½ oz) potato starch
- 150 g (5 oz) flour
- 6 egg whites
- 75 g (2 ½ oz) sugar

Preheat the oven to gas mark 6 (200°C, 400°F). Beat the egg yolks with 150 g (5 oz) sugar. Sieve the potato starch with the flour. Whisk the egg whites with 75 g (3 oz) sugar. Add a little of the stiff egg white to the yolk mixture then pour the yolk mixture back into the whites. Fold in the flour and potato starch, taking care when mixing not to beat out any air. Using a piping bag and a 16mm (½ in) diameter nozzle, pipe out finger shapes 10 to 12 cm (4 to 5 in) long on to a greased and floured baking tray. Sprinkle with icing sugar. Bake for 10 to 12 minutes until the icing sugar begins to bubble on the surface and the biscuit is becoming firm to the touch. Lift the biscuits off the baking tray and allow to cool.

**RECIPE
ROLLET PRADIER**

CHOCOLATE CHARLOTTE

First, prepare the chocolate custard. Soak the gelatine in cold water, and bring the milk to the boil. Whisk the egg yolks and sugar until pale in colour. Grate the chocolate into a bowl and add the cocoa. Stirring continuously, pour the boiling milk on to the egg yolk mixture, place it back in the pan and bring back to the boil over a low heat. Remove from the heat and continue to stir for a few minutes. Add the strained gelatine and pour the hot mixture over the chocolate to melt it. Leave to cool. Prepare the mould by placing biscuits in the base and vertically around the sides, reserving a few biscuits for the base of the charlotte. Combine the cooled chocolate custard with the whipped cream, pour into the mould, and finish by laying a few biscuits on the top. Refrigerate for 3 hours before turning out of the mould by first immersing it in hot water. Serve accompanied by vanilla custard.

Ingredients for 8 servings:
- ½ litre (18 fl. oz) milk
- 3 egg yolks
- 75 g (3 oz) sugar
- 25 g (1 oz) cocoa powder
- 125 g (4 ½ oz) bitter 66 per cent cocoa cooking chocolate
- 3 sheets leaf gelatine
- 250 g (9 oz) whipped cream
- 1 charlotte mould 180 mm (7 in) diameter
- finger biscuits (see opposite)

VANILLA CUSTARD

Split the vanilla pod and scrape some of the seeds into the milk and bring to the boil. Whisk the egg yolks and sugar together until pale in colour. Pour the boiling milk on to the egg yolk mixture, stirring all the time. Place back in the pan, bring to the boil over a low heat; remove from the heat and continue stirring for a few minutes. Pour into a serving bowl and leave to cool.

Ingredients for 8 servings:
- ½ litre (1 ¾ pt) milk
- 4 egg yolks
- 125 g (4 ½ oz) sugar
- 1 vanilla pod

Brownies and Sachertorte

BROWNIES

Originating in the United States, the brownie has conquered the whole world. It is made with walnuts, or more traditionally with pecan nuts. Serve with custard (see page 95).

Preheat the oven to gas mark 4 (180°C, 350°F). Melt the chocolate and butter in a bain-marie. In a mixing bowl combine the eggs and sugar, then pour in the melted chocolate. Gradually fold in the flour, corn oil and baking powder. Add the nuts. Mix until well incorporated. Grease a rectangular cake tin. Pour in the mixture. Bake in the oven for 35 minutes. Turn out and serve warm.

Preparation time: 20 min
Cooking time: 35 min

Ingredients for 6 servings:
• 150 g (5 oz) plain chocolate
• 80 g (3 oz) butter
• 2 eggs
• 150 g (5 oz) caster sugar
• 100 g (3 ½ oz) plain flour
• 30 g (1 fl. oz) corn oil
• ½ teaspoon baking powder
• 100 g (3 ½ oz) walnut pieces, roughly chopped

SACHERTORTE

The recipe for Sachertorte is reputed to have originated in the Sacher Hotel in Vienna in 1852. A subtle marriage of chocolate and apricot preserve, it is sometimes accompanied by a bowl of whipped cream.

Preheat the oven to gas mark 4 (180°C, 350°F). Separate the eggs. Melt 120 g (4 ½ oz) chocolate in a bain-marie. Beat the egg yolks and the caster sugar together until quite pale, then add the melted butter and the chocolate and stir. Whisk the egg whites into stiff peaks with 40 g (1 ½ oz) sugar, fold lightly into the mixture, lifting to aerate. Add the flour and mix well. Butter a cake tin and spoon in the cake mixture. Bake in the oven for 35 to 40 minutes. Leave to cool, then turn out and slice lengthways into two. Sandwich the two halves together with 150 g (5 oz) apricot jam. Heat the rest of the jam and spread over the outside of the cake. Put to one side. Break the chocolate into pieces and place with the icing sugar and water into a bain-marie. Gently melt,

Preparation time: 1 hour
Cooking time for the cake: 40 min
Refrigeration time: 30 min

Ingredients for 6 to 8 servings:
• 120 g (4 ½ oz) plain chocolate
• 120 g (4 ½ oz) softened butter
• 6 eggs
• 170 g (6 oz) caster sugar
• 120 g (4 ½ oz) plain flour
• 250 g (9 oz) apricot jam

For the glaze:
• 370 g (13 oz) plain chocolate
• 180 g (6 oz) icing sugar
• 10 cl (3 ½ oz) water

mixing until smooth. Place the cake on a wire tray and pour the chocolate glaze over the surface and the sides. Smooth and leave to set. The Sachertorte is ready to eat when the coating has hardened.

Roast turkey with Mole Poblano sauce

The popular story behind this recipe is that in the 16th century an archbishop visited the Santa Rosa convent in Puebla, Mexico, with the intention of sampling their famous cooking. Panic-stricken, the nuns prayed for inspiration. They roasted a turkey and to accompany it they blended together a mixture of pimentos, almonds, tomatoes, garlic, bread, tortillas and bananas. To add a little originality, they added some bitter chocolate. They had just invented Mole Poblano, a sauce laced with chocolate. However, the recipe probably goes back much further, since a similar sauce is said to have been served to the Aztec king Montezuma.

MOLE POBLANO

Roast a chicken or turkey. Meanwhile cut the chillies in half, removing the stem and seeds. Soak for one hour in boiling water. Drain and put in a blender with all the spices and the tortilla, and blend into a paste. In a saucepan heat the oil, then add the mixture and brown it. Gradually add the water, then the chicken stock and stir well. Simmer for 1 hour over a low heat. Add the pieces of chocolate and 2 pinches of salt. Continue cooking gently for one more hour. Serve with the roast turkey or chicken.

Preparation time: 10 min
Cooking time: 2 hours on a low heat
• 10 dried or preserved chilli peppers
• 500 ml (18 fl oz) chicken stock
• 50 ml (18 fl oz) water
• 2 chopped garlic cloves
• 5 teaspoons almonds
• 3 peeled and chopped tomatoes
• 1 tablespoon raisins
• 1 fried tortilla, cut into pieces
• 2 teaspoons sesame seeds
• 1 teaspoon fresh coriander
• 2 cloves
• 1 teaspoon cinnamon
• 30 g (1 oz) bitter-sweet chocolate
• 4 teaspoons peanut oil
• salt

FIND OUT

CHOCOLATE, THE EU AND THE LAW.
TASTING AND APPRECIATING CHOCOLATE AS WINE.
THE LINKS BETWEEN CHOCOLATE AND SENSUALITY.
PAIRING ALCOHOL WITH CHOCOLATE.
SUBLIME INSPIRATION FOR ARTISTS AND CRAFTSMEN.
USEFUL ADDRESSES TO FIND OUT MORE.

The writer's love of chocolate

What did Madame de Sévigné, Casanova and the Marquis de Sade have in common? They were all sensual people, who loved chocolate, writing about it either directly or through their characters.

In James Runcie's *The Discovery of Chocolate*, the Spaniard Diego de Godoy travels across the world and through time in search of the perfect chocolate and his beloved Ignacia. The story begins in 1518, when Diego joins Cortés' conquistadors and meets Ignacia. When Diego returns to Spain, Ignacia sends him on his way with a chocolate drink, the elixir of life. She assures him that 'If you are alive, then I am alive. Never cease in your search for me.' But he returns to find her dead, and then begins 'an eternity of travel'. On his way he meets, among others, the Marquis de Sade, with whom he discusses chocolate. After many encounters with famous historical figures, and many adventures, the story ends as Diego returns to Mexico in the 1900s.

There's a happy ending in Roald Dahl's story, *Charlie and the Chocolate Factory*. Charlie Bucket's family is poor and his father does not earn enough to buy luxuries. Charlie, a growing boy, 'wanted something more filling and satisfying than cabbage and cabbage soup. The one thing he longed for more than anything else was... chocolate .... Only once a year, on his birthday, ... Charlie was always presented with one small chocolate bar to eat all by himself. ... he would place it carefully in a small wooden box that he owned, and treasure it as though it were a bar of solid gold; and for the next few days, he would allow himself only to look at it, but never to touch it. Then at last, when he could stand it no longer,(...) he would take a tiny nibble – just enough to allow the lovely sweet taste to spread out slowly over his tongue. The next day, he would take another tiny nibble, and so on, and so on. And in this way, Charlie would make his sixpenny bar of birthday chocolate last him for more than a month.' Not only did Charlie have to endure this awful state of affairs, he also had to suffer a much greater torture. 'In the town itself, ... there was an enormous chocolate factory!(...) It was owned by a man called Mr Willy Wonka, the greatest inventor and maker of chocolates, that there has ever been. ... And outside the walls, for half a mile around in every direction, the air was scented with the heavy rich smell of melting chocolate!' Charlie would look desperately at the factory entrance without being able to go in. However, one day, Willy Wonka announced there was to be a hunt for five golden tickets to visit the factory and Charlie is one of the lucky winners. After many adventures, he triumphs over the other children and wins his ultimate dream. Today there are many captivating stories about chocolate for children, but few works on the subject written for adults. As with the 17th-century *Letters* of Madame de Sévigné, several of which follow the vagaries of the drink's fashionability, the large majority of writers who have included snippets about chocolate in their writings have done so because of its importance in their particular era.

Throughout his works, the great chocolate lover, Casanova, missed no opportunity to wax lyrical on the subject. Chocolate was used as an alibi for his amorous adventures in *Histoire de ma vie*

(History of my life), and as a device for political comment on France in *Mon apprentissage à Paris* (My apprenticeship in Paris). 'The French Nation can at present be likened to gunpowder, or chocolate; both are composed of three ingredients; their quality can, and does, only depend on the dosage. Only time will tell which ingredients were superfluous before the Revolution, and which are superfluous now. All that I can say is that the stink of sulphur is fatal, and that vanilla is a poison.' Another controversial character, the Marquis de Sade, used chocolate to gratify the amorous energies or the murderous intent of his characters. In *Les Infortunes de la vertu* (The misfortunes of virtue), Monsieur de Bressac, wishing to benefit as quickly as possible from his mother's fortune, asks Sophie to put poison in her daily chocolate. The famous German traveller Alexander von Humboldt extolled the virtues of chocolate, saying that 'on no other occasion apart from this specific instance, has nature concentrated in so small a space such an abundance of the most valuable nourishment'. In *Les Terres du bout du monde* (The lands at the ends of the earth) and *Cacao,* Jorge Amado, born in 1912 on a cocoa plantation south of Bahia, described the pitiful conditions endured by people living in the cocoa plantations at the beginning of the 20th century. It follows the struggle of a small group of cocoa growers trying to make their fortune. To the farmers, cocoa is a prize well worth fighting for. Fighting breaks out in the group, resulting in several murders. In the more contemporary novel, *Chocolat,* Joanne Harris explores the well-worn theme of chocolate representing gluttony with the consequent loss of morality. The forces of Good and Evil, embodied in the two main characters, are pitched against each other. When Vianne Rocher opens her wonderfully fragrant chocolate shop, *La Céleste Praline,* opposite the church in Lanquenest-sur-Tannes, she provokes the anger of Francis Reynaud, the parish priest. Gradually, Reynaud loses his influence over his parishioners, who can't resist the selection of hot chocolate, florentines, white rum truffles, 'mendiants' etc. in Rocher's shop. One day he discovers her plan to organize a 'Festival du chocolat' on Easter Sunday. It is the last straw, and the priest condemns her actions in his sermon. Threatening hell and damnation, warning against temptation, he declares: 'Church, not Chocolate.' Tormented by memories of his sordid past, and sensing Rocher's imminent triumph, Francis Reynaud breaks into *La Céleste Praline* in the early hours of Easter Sunday, aiming to destroy everything on display, but he is bewitched by the tempting chocolates. He gorges on them until he can eat no more, at which point Rocher discovers him, banishes him back to his church, where he becomes a broken man.

Is chocolate a suitable subject for an adult novel?

It would seem so. Joanne Harris's *Chocolat*, was also released as a film starring Juliette Binoche, Judi Dench and Johnny Depp to rave reviews.

'A tale guaranteed to titillate the palate and lend sustenance to the heart ... a romantic, playfully rebellious, lush and ultimately moving spirit that makes *Chocolat* as tempting as chocolate itself ... a hopeful celebration of all the sweeter things in life.' (*The Scotsman*).

'This delicious, bewitching novel provides the antidote to all those late 20th-century body shape obsessions; to all those tired and tiring Bridget Jones stereotypes. Here's a story, written by a woman, that celebrates chocolate *without guilt*!' (*Scotland on Sunday*).

'Bitter and sweet bite into one another, balance each other. It's a delicious read, witchy and decadent. Sumptuous descriptions of bonbons and cakes slink across the page, hints of magic and evil. The result is a sly contest between feast and fast.' (*Time Out*).

The EU has its say

To earn the definition of plain or dark chocolate, a product must contain a minimum of 35 per cent total dry cocoa solids, of which 18 per cent must be cocoa butter and 14 per cent dry cocoa mass. Milk chocolate must contain a minimum of 25 per cent total dry cocoa solids. A maximum of five per cent vegetable fats is now permitted in addition to cocoa butter.

The saga of the EU declaring that much of British chocolate had no legal right to call itself 'chocolate' as it was not pure enough caused enormous upset and indignation in the industry a few years ago. However, on 15 March 2000 the European Parliament decreed that it is now possible to add 5 per cent vegetable fats of tropical origin other than cocoa butter to the recipe for chocolate. The permitted oils are illipe, sal, shea nut, palm, mango kernel and kokum gurgi. France, Belgium, Italy, Germany, Holland, Luxembourg and Spain fought to maintain what they saw as the purity of their chocolate, but in 1996 the European Commission decided to revise the 1973 cocoa-chocolate directive in order to standardise the definition of chocolate in force in member states. Only the United Kingdom, Ireland and Denmark were at that time authorised by their own national legislation to manufacture chocolate containing five per cent vegetable fats. The other states were still making pure chocolate from cocoa, sugar and cocoa butter, although it was permitted for manufacturers to add a little soya lecithin. This additive, unrecognisable except to purists, stabilises the chocolate's consistency.

As new countries have joined the European Union, the proportion of traditional chocolate supporters has decreased. Portugal, Austria, Sweden and Finland obtained the right to introduce 5 per cent vegetable fats into their chocolate without any special dispensation. This new directive allows free movement of chocolate goods in Europe. The multinationals (Ferrero, Nestlé, Kraft-Jacob-Suchard, Cadbury) are no longer required to alter their manufacturing processes for different countries. They can, therefore, gain new markets and make considerable savings. The substituted vegetable fats cost two per cent less than cocoa butter, which represents nine per cent of the total cost of the chocolate.

This change in the law threatens to redraw the map of cocoa production, and the cocoa producing countries have no choice but to go along with it. Although the figure of five per cent reduction in cocoa butter seems relatively small, it could amount to a loss in trade of 200,000 tonnes of cocoa and the fall in world prices could be close to 15 to 20 per cent. The first to suffer would be the biggest cocoa growers such as Nigeria, Cameroon and the Ivory Coast. However, countries such as Mali, which sell shea nut oil at a third of the price of cocoa butter, would stand to gain, as would the regions that produce cheap palm oil. From a technical point of view, vegetable fats improve the snap, gloss and heat resistance of chocolate, so it is possible both to improve the quality of commercial chocolate and to create new chocolate products by introducing supplementary fats. Many Continental producers fear that this will mark the end of 'real' chocolate, but in the opinion of both commercial and specialist chocolate makers, the demand for high-quality chocolate continues to grow. In the words of Sylvain Margou, general secretary of the National Union of French Chocolate Makers: 'You don't stop making a good recipe. Enthusiasts will go on enjoying pure chocolate.' Just as there are already chocolate products with and without the addition of soya lecithin, so there will be chocolate products with and without vegetable fats. The serious chocolate-lover who wants to keep an eye on the chocolateyness of the chocolate he or she is about to eat will have to patronise the specialist chocolate-makers and check the wrapper when buying chocolate from supermarket shelves. In the words of a British MEP at the time of the vote in March 2000: 'People are not stupid and can tell the difference between different types of chocolate.' QED.

Chocolate appreciation as an art

Chocolate is not treated like any ordinary delicacy. Perhaps it is because it was known as the 'food of the gods' that this former treasure of the Aztecs has given rise to all sorts of rituals throughout the world.

In terms of tasting, chocolate can easily be compared with wine, and a similar element of snobbishness can hover around the appreciation of chocolate. Indeed, the terms used to define quality and character come from the same vocabulary as wine appreciation. In addition, there is a certain ritual involved in becoming an enlightened enthusiast, or an experienced chocolate buff. Place two white plates on a table covered with a plain, light-coloured tablecloth. In the middle of the first put a block of solid chocolate, on the other a single, individual chocolate with a soft filling. Using both hands, break the block of chocolate in two, pressing with the thumbs. The 'snap' of the chocolate is assessed – good quality chocolate should make a clean, precise break. Another indicator of quality is a smooth, glossy appearance. The colour should be intense and pleasing – brown with amber tones, a brownish-purple or mahogany – reflecting the colour of the cocoa beans, dried and roasted to perfection, and the hot, sun-soaked earth of the country of origin. Smell the chocolate, then place it in the mouth for the final test. In a good quality block of plain dark chocolate there should be no hint of graininess as it melts and coats the inside of the mouth. The attack should contain subtle acidity, followed by a gradual increase in bitterness and, depending on the origin of the cocoa, as with wine, the finish can be one of smoky or floral notes, or flavours of red fruit.

Now taste the individual chocolate, but refresh your taste buds with a piece of white bread or a glass of water. With one hand, hold the single chocolate between thumb and index finger. Take a narrow-bladed knife in the other hand and slice the chocolate in half. There should be no crumbs or splinters, the coating should be as fine as possible with a delicate crispness. In the mouth, it should vanish almost instantly, giving way to the filling (ganache, praline, cream, etc.) beneath the scents of cocoa. There should be no excessive sweetness or acidity, no sourness, or bitter, burnt, rancid or musty taste. Balance and finesse are the words to use; flavours should mingle in the mouth in waves, or contrast with each other with carefully orchestrated subtlety. Those first intense flavours may startle, or the exquisitely blended taste may even intoxicate, but a good chocolate will never fail to impress.

Vocabulary describing chocolate can be likened to that of wine, and can be just as bizarre. Here are a few of the terms used by expert tasters.

Visual assessment

Appearance: matt, glossy, silky, smooth, grainy, powdery, dull, blotchy, marked.

Smell and taste

Flowers: Jasmine, violet.
Fruits: raspberry, blackcurrant, cherry, pear, quince, candied fruits, red berries, prune.
Zest: lemon, orange.
Pungency: burnt, smoky, roast almonds or hazelnuts, toast, tobacco, hay, roasted flavours (cocoa bean), Havana.
Spices: saffron, clove, vanilla, pepper.
Vegetation: earthy, cut grass, truffle, undergrowth, stable smell or taste.

Touch

Texture in the mouth: mellow, supple, melting, soft, fine, clean, dense, crumbly, floury, powdery, granular, light, greasy.

Character

Elegant, racy, fruity, floral, scented, aromatic, fragrant, structured, well-balanced, earthy, heavy, ordinary, exclusive, neutral, insipid, poor. Pleasant, classic, exotic, satisfying, luxurious, sensual, erotic, unpleasant, dull, pedantic, pretentious, brash, superficial, bland.

Obsession!

Chocoholic or *chocomaniac*, from *chocomania*, refers to being totally dependant on chocolate.

Drinks to accompany chocolate

The bitter-sweet flavour of chocolate does not mix well with alcoholic drinks. However, some combinations are possible.

Forget dry white wine and dry champagne, because their acidity destroys the softness and subtlety of some chocolate and fruit combinations. Nevertheless, a full-bodied pink champagne with its hints of red berry fruits does go well with a chocolate and raspberry sponge. You could also go for a lighter, sparkling red from the Loire. The younger classic Bordeaux and Burgundys are definitely out of the question, as their tannins intensify the bitterness of cocoa. A light red wine, served chilled (Saumur-Champigny, red Sancerre or Beaujolais) will give a distinctive touch to a dark chocolate dessert. Very sweet dessert wines (Sauternes, Monbazillac, Jurançon) will swamp tastebuds still savouring the sweet delights of a chocolate dessert. The only appropriate partner for chocolate is a fortified wine (Spanish sherry, Macvin de Jura, Pineau des Charentes, Floc de Gascogne, Rivesaltes, Banyuls or a port), or a spirit (an armagnac, cognac or whisky). To a greater or lesser extent and depending on their age, liqueurs and fortified wines have a taste of raisins, roasted hazelnuts, cocoa, prunes, apricots or nutty oak. The strong, dry character of a spirit will bring out the strong flavour of cocoa. Served at a temperature of 12°C (54°F), there is nothing to beat a Banyuls with a pistachio-cream pie, a Maury with a plain and milk chocolate mousse, or a Rivesaltes with a walnut and chocolate cake. Cointreau that complements a chocolate orange dessert, or a pear liqueur to accompany a pear and chocolate pastry should be served chilled at 6 to 8°C (43–46°F). Room temperature is preferable for a cognac served with a 70 per cent cocoa dark chocolate ganache. Nor is there a problem with a Macvin de Jura to go with a white chocolate mousse, provided that it is kept at a temperature of 8–10°C (46–50°F).

In cookery, some unusual dishes pair up well with chocolate sauces, such as red mullet. A Chateauneuf-du-Pape, mellowed with age, is a suitable accompaniment for hare in chocolate sauce. Roast chicken in a slightly piquant chocolate sauce is enhanced by the warm notes of a Spanish Rioja or a peppery Croze-Hermitage (Côtes du Rhône). Pork fillet with smoky bacon in a gravy combined with melted dark chocolate will find its match in a red Costières de Nîmes.

On chocolate...

'I'm mad about Chocolat Lanvin', Salvador Dali, painter.
"When I die," I said to my friend, "I'm not going to be embalmed, I'm going to be dipped." "Milk or bittersweet?" was her immediate concern. This is the rhetorical response of one chocolate addict to another. We both know the answer. Bittersweet.' Adrienne Marcus, The Chocolate Bible.
'Katherine Hepburn, 70, actress, asked how she stays trim: "I don't have to watch my figure as I never had much of one to watch. What you see is the result of a lifetime of chocolate."' Time Magazine, 17 November 1980.
'The chocolate bar is an edible American flag, a security blanket for the distraut, a barometer of a nation's economic health.' New York Times, 25 February 1979.
In The Clandestine Marriage *by George Colman and David Garrick, Act II opens with two servants stealing sips of their master's chocolate. The chambermaid says, "Tis very fine indeed! – and charmingly perfumed – it smells for all the world like our young ladies' dressing boxes.'*
'Caramels are a fad, chocolate is a permanent thing.' Milton Snavely Hershey.

Plain, milk or white, the best chocolate is the one you prefer

The higher the percentage of cocoa, the better the chocolate.

Wrong. With a cocoa content above 75 per cent the bitterness is so pronounced – unless it is perfectly controlled – that it overwhelms all the other nuances of flavour. In addition, a high percentage of cocoa can sometimes mask the taste of poor quality beans (inadequately fermented, dried or roasted). An excellent chocolate that contains 55 per cent cocoa tastes far better than a poor chocolate with 70 per cent.

You can only taste the true intensity of plain chocolate in solid block chocolate.

Not true. You can discover all the subtleties of cocoa in a block of plain chocolate, and it's also interesting to compare cocoas of different origins to get a complete picture of the infinite range of aromas in chocolate. On the other hand, assorted chocolates reveal their complex, refined flavours much more slowly, first through the chocolate coating (often a blend of several couvertures), and then through the fillings, which are often rich in cocoa and other ingredients.

Is true chocolate plain chocolate?

No. Chocolate can be enjoyed in a variety of different forms. There is a chocolate for every moment of the day. A well-made milk chocolate combines the bitter notes of cocoa with the smoothness of milk and caramel flavours. A block of fruit and nut chocolate is the perfect combination of crunchy nuts, soft, melting chocolate and the flavour of dried fruit. A plain chocolate containing 75 per cent cocoa can pack a powerful punch. A true quality chocolate is simply one that tempts you, and as long as it is fresh, it is one that you will enjoy.

Is pure chocolate better than chocolate containing other vegetable fats?

As far as the purists are concerned there is no doubt. Chocolate containing other vegetable fats has a slightly waxy texture and is oily. It does not have the same intensity on the tongue as 'pure cocoa'. But let's be honest, if it's a chocolate with a sufficiently high cocoa content (between 60 and 75 per cent) that has been well made, it is quite difficult to taste the difference between other vegetable fats and cocoa butter. The only solution for the consumer is to read the packaging carefully to distinguish between a pure cocoa chocolate and one with added vegetable fats.

Should I keep chocolate in the refrigerator?

Absolutely not. The cold moisture breaks and alters the texture and as with all fats, cocoa butter can be tainted by other odours. Whatever the type of chocolate, it is best kept in a cool, dry place, well wrapped and away from light. Once opened it is best to eat a bar of chocolate within a fortnight, and a box of handmade, filled chocolates within a week, in order to take full advantage of their freshness and aroma.

Chocolate has inspired artists and craftsmen

The practice of chocolate-drinking inspired 18th-century potters to create beautiful porcelain cups and chocolate pots. Artists depicted chocolate-lovers in the act of sipping their favourite tipple. With the rise in advertising, all the big chocolate manufacturers called in the best poster-artists. Packaging designers displayed chocolate in magnificent boxes, and it has even been incorporated into high couture garments.

As it became more accepted into society and more widely available, the enjoyment of chocolate grew. Since the 16th century the passion surrounding chocolate has been interpreted in many ways. Both manufacturers and enthusiasts have given chocolate a strong identity. Every discipline in the art world has portrayed or used chocolate at some time or other. Drinking chocolate became a symbol of courtly behaviour and aristocratic sociability via the noble ladies at the Spanish court. It was the golden age of porcelain design, and craftsmen created magnificent chocolate pots and exquisite cups as befitted such an exclusive and divine drink. One of them was Augustin de Saint-Aubin, royal engraver and a master of decorative design, who created a chocolate service for Madame du Barry produced by the Sèvres factory near Paris.

These moments of epicurean indulgence became a regular subject for contemporary paintings. Still-life paintings depicted the objects associated with the pleasure of drinking chocolate. In 1776 the Spanish artist Luis Meléndez painted a chocolate pot and a few scattered brioches. Some years earlier

Antonio de Pereda y Salgado had painted an arrangement of objects used in the drinking of chocolate. Chocolate was frequently incorporated into portraits and scenes of family life, as in paintings by the artists Jean-François de Troy (1679–1752) and Jean-Baptiste Greuze (1725–1805). *La Belle Chocolatière* (the beautiful chocolate pot) (1743) and *Le Petit Déjeuner* (breakfast) (1754) by Jean-Etienne Liotard depict morning chocolate drinking. *Le Déjeuner* (lunch) (1739) by François Boucher, and *La Tasse de chocolat* (the cup of chocolate) or *Le Duc de Penthièvre et sa famille* (the Duke of Penthièvre and his family) by Louis-Michel Van Loo (1770–71) feature chocolate drinking as a family activity. In stark contrast, Hogarth's famous series of pictures, the 'Rake's Progress', includes a scene from White's Coffee House, a famous chocolate house, which evolved into a gentleman's club. Gambling and dissipation were characteristic of chocolate houses of the day, and Hogarth reflects the atmosphere in graphic detail. Chocolate even made an appearance in the world of music – in Mozart's opera, *Così fan tutte*, the maid, Despina, cannot resist it, and takes a forbidden sip of the chocolate she is required to make.

'This young gallant and this beautiful lady are enjoying a cup of chocolate, but one can see such ardent passion in their eyes that one would think they needed a more delicate refreshment.'

Fashion show at the
Salon Du Chocolat,
1998. The model
wears a dress of
steel and chocolate
by Paco Rabanne.

As time progressed and technological advances meant that chocolate could be produced in new forms, from being an exclusive preserve of the elite it became part of everyone's lives. The heyday of poster advertising added to its popularity. Manufacturers were fascinated by this new art style, and Fry among others produced many fine examples. One poster shows a smiling girl walking through the snow as her dog scampers ahead with a box of chocolates in its mouth. The lettering says: 'Fry's milk chocolate & pure concentrated cocoa. Going by leaps & bounds.' One of Fry's best-known posters depicts five portraits of a small boy. Captioned 'The Story of Fry's Chocolate', it shows the boy's successive expressions, 'Desperation' is followed by 'Pacification', 'Expectation', 'Acclamation. and finally 'Realisation'. "It's Fry's." Chocolate became inextricably linked with temptation and was delicately packaged in beautiful boxes. The first containers were made of lithographed metal, then improvements in technology brought the advent of cardboard boxes. Richard Cadbury introduced the first British-made chocolate boxes, decorated with his own pictures of his children, holiday scenes or flowers. Other chocolate-makers drew inspiration for the box designs from Asia, famous battles, or works by artists from Van Gogh to Lautrec.

Once a year, on the opening day of the Salon du Chocolat (Chocolate Show)in Paris, Sylvie Douce and François Jeantet hold a very special fashion show, during which well-known designers add an unusual dimension to the world of fashion. On the catwalk in 1999 among others was a dress made exclusively from CDs and steel by Courrèges for Madame de Sévigné, a dress in steel and chocolate by Paco Rabanne for Richard, a chocolate cape by Sherrer for Thuriez, a wasp-waisted corset by Chantal Thomas for Christian Constant ... and a wedding dress made by Catherine Puget for the Foucher chocolate house. Protected in special temperature-controlled trunks, all these sumptuous clothes were flown across the Atlantic to the Chocolate Show in New York at Thanksgiving, and then on to the St Valentine's chocolate exhibition in Tokyo.

Are you a chocolate buff?
Try our chocolate quiz

TRUE OR FALSE

1 • All the world's cacao trees originate from a single species, the criollo.
❏ True   ❏ False

2 • The forestero bean is the source for commercial chocolate.
❏ True   ❏ False

3 • The island of Trinidad exports 1,200 tonnes of cocoa per year.
❏ True   ❏ False

4 • Cocoa is the result of fermenting and drying cocoa beans.
❏ True   ❏ False

5 • Cocoa mass contains dry cocoa solids and cocoa butter.
❏ True   ❏ False

6 • Conching consists of grinding cocoa and cocoa butter to make chocolate smoother.
❏ True   ❏ False

7 • The British eat 2 kg (4.4 lb) chocolate per person per year.
❏ True   ❏ False

8 • Americans eat the most chocolate.
❏ True   ❏ False

9 • The Swiss eat 10.16 kg (2.35 lb) chocolate per person per year.
❏ True   ❏ False

10 • The French prefer solid block chocolate to chocolate bars.
❏ True   ❏ False

11 • Gianduja is an individual chocolate filled with nougat.
❏ True   ❏ False

12 • Ganache is made from chocolate and cream.
❏ True   ❏ False

QUIZ

1 • Spotting a ship off the coast in 1519, King Montezuma believed that the prophecy of Quetzalcoatl was coming true. The ship's captain was:
a • Christopher Columbus
b • Hernan Cortés
c • Vasco da Gama

2 • In 1527 chocolate made its first appearance in which royal court?
a • Spain
b • France
c • England

3 • Which of these queens introduced chocolate to France?
a • Marie de Médici
b • Anne of Austria
c • Marie-Thérèse of Austria

4 • The first chocolate shop opened in London in:
a • 1656
b • 1657
c • 1671

5 • Who developed the process for making cocoa powder?
a • Coenraad van Houten
b • Joseph Fry
c • Victor-Auguste Poulain

6 • Valrhona launched its 100 per cent pure range of chocolate, 'grands crus', on an industrial scale in the year:
a • 1983
b • 1984
c • 1985

7 • In 1734 cocoa was given the scientific name, Theobroma, by whom?
a • The doctor, Juan de Cardenas
b • The naturalist, Carolus Linnaeus
c • Doctor Theo Broma

8 • The name of the London chocolate house which became a famous gentleman's club was:
a • Brown's
b • The Kit Kat Club
c • White's

9 • In 1997 cocoa production was estimated at:
a • 2.2 million tonnes
   b • 2.6 million tonnes
      c • 2.8 million tonnes

10 • The Ivory Coast, top cocoa grower, produces in total:
a • 1 million tonnes
b • 1.08 million tonnes
c • 1.1 million tonnes

11 • To get one tonne of dried cocoa beans it takes a harvest of:
a • 15,000 pods
b • 25,000 pods
c • 35,000 pods

12 • 'Nacional' cocoa, produced in Ecuador, comes from which bean?
a • Criollo
b • Forestero
c • Trinitario

Specialist chocolatiers

▼

GREAT BRITAIN

BETTYS AND TAYLORS
Pagoda House
Plumpton Park
Harrogate
Tel: 0845 345 3636
Indulgent chocolates made by Lucerne-trained staff. Products include their Swiss-inspired Chocolate Desires.

CHARBONNEL ET WALKER
The Royal Arcade
28 Old Bond Street
London W1X 4BT
Tel: 0207 491 0939
English flavours and French methods. Don't miss it.

THE CHOCOLATE SOCIETY SHOP
36 Elizabeth Street
London SW1
Tel: 0207 259 9222
A mecca for chocolate connoisseurs.

L'ATELIER DU CHOCOLAT
Unit 25
Elbourne Trading Estate
Crabtree Manorway
South
Belvedere, Kent
Tel: 0208 311 3337
Freshly-made chocolates made with a range of ingredients, including honey, nuts, candied peels and cinnamon.

NEUHAUS BELGIAN CHOCOLATES
3 Roslin Square
Roslin Road
Acton
London W3 8BY
Tel: 0208 993 6956
Belgian chocolates on sale in London.

ROCOCO
321 King's Road
London SW3 5EP
Tel: 0207 352 5857
Chocolates created by Chantal Coady, one of the new generation of British chocolatiers.

THORNTONS
Thornton Park
Somercotes
Derbyshire DE55 4JX
Tel: 01773 540550
Branches throughout Britain.

PARIS

LA MAISON DU CHOCOLAT
225 Rue du Faubourg-Saint-Honoré
75008 Paris
Tel: 00 33 1 42 27 39 44
Robert Linxe, supreme chocolatier, needs no introduction. He concocts chocolates like Verdi, Gounod or Puccini composed their music. Melt at the thought of a Rigoletto, Faust, Traviata or Bohème.

CHRISTIAN CONSTANT
37 Rue d'Assas
75006 Paris
Tel: 00 33 1 53 63 15 15
Pure poetry created by the finest couvertures and a whole range of ganache flavours, from rose and currant, through jasmine and green tea, to Tahitian vanilla or orange blossom. Which one will tempt you?

JEAN-PAUL HÉVIN
231 Rue Saint-Honoré
75008 Paris
Tel: 00 33 1 55 35 35 96
The only one of his kind, Jean-Paul creates unusual chocolate combinations according to whim, such as camembert chocolate. Or why not try a more traditional honey, rum-and-raisin, ginger or raspberry ganache?

ITALY

MAJANI
Via del Carbonesi 5
Bologna
Tel: 00 39 0 51 234 302
Home of Cremino Fiat, an assorted chocolate with alternating layers of almond chocolate and hazelnut and chocolate, created for the launch of a new Fiat in 1911.

PEYRANO
Corsa Moncalieri 47
Turin
Tel: 00 39 0 116 60 22 02
According to the people of Turin this is the best place to buy gianduja. Also discover bicerin, a chocolate, hazelnut and honey spread that adds flavour to coffee.

BELGIUM

GODIVA
Grand-Place 22
Brussels
Tel: 00 32 0 2 511 25 37
www.godiva.com
In case you have never tried one of these internationally renowned pralines.

LÉONIDAS
Boulevard Anspach 46
Brussels
Tel: 00 32 0 2 218 03 63
www.leonidas.com
Try 'Manon' coated in white chocolate, one of the large variety of pralines.

Where to eat and drink chocolate

GREAT BRITAIN

GODIVA
247 Regent Street
London W1B 2EW
Tel: 020 7647 9705
Mainly a Godiva 'boutique' for buying chocolate products, but there's room for a couple of chairs and a hot chocolate machine.

THE CHOCOLATE SOCIETY
36 Elizabeth Street
London SW1W 9NZ
Tel: 020 7259 9222
In the heart of London's Belgravia, this is another shop that manages to squeeze a couple of tables on to its premises and serve coffee and chocolate.

FRANCE

GÉRARD MULOT
76 Rue de Seine
75006 Paris
Tel: 00 33 1 43 26 85 77
In the middle of fashionable Saint-Germain-des Prés where

the chocolate cream pastry, Magie-Noire (black magic), is made.

FAUCHON
26–30 Place de la Madeleine
75008 Paris
Tel: 00 33 1 47 42 60
Among other desserts to try is l'Auguste, a chocolate speciality flavoured with tea, Provençal honey, Java pepper, morello cherries, or Zimbabwean coffee.

LENÔTRE
44 Rue d'Auteuil
75016 Paris
Tel: 00 33 1 45 24 52 52
Delicious chocolate tarts, pastries and cakes.

L'HEURE GOURMANDE
22 Passage Dauphine
Paris
Tel: 00 33 1 46 34 00 40
A quiet place for long conversations over white porcelain cups filled with an elegant strong chocolate.

ITALY

CAFFE BARATTI & MILANO
Piazza Castello 29
Turin
Tel: 00 39 1 15 61 30 60
Surrounded by wood and mirrors, next to the Regio theatre, how can you resist a hot chocolate or a handful of truffles?

RIVOIRE
Piazza della Signora 41
Florence
Tel: 00 39 0 55 214 412
Situated in the beautiful city of Florence, the Café Rivoire was established in 1871 by a family of confectioners from Haute-Savoie. Gain strength from a delectable cup of hot chocolate before buying a pot of crema cioccolato, a chocolate spread for utter indulgence.

GERMANY

KÖNIG
Lichtentaler Strasse 2
Baden-Baden
Tel: 00 49 7221 235 73
Try a traditional hot chocolate in this temple of German gastronomy.

AUSTRIA

LEHMANN
Graben 12
U-bahn Stephansplatz
Vienna
Tel: 00 43 512 18 18
A popular and elegant Konditorei (patisserie), serving pastries made with chocolate, cream, and icing.

CAFÉ SACHER
1 Philharmonikerstrasse 4
A-1010 Vienna
Tel: 00 43 512 14 87
Tourists love this café, with its rich décor of red and gold, and portraits on the walls. The renowned cake, Sachertorte, is served here, made to a recipe that is still based on the original.

Make sure you know how to ask for chocolate when abroad

China
tchyaokeuli

Denmark
chokolade

France
chocolat

Germany
Schokolade

Greece
sokolata

Holland
chocolaad

Italy
cioccolato

Norway
sjokolade

Poland
zsekolada

Russia
chokolad

Spain and Portugal
chocolate

Sweden
choklad

Turkey
pikolata

Exhibitions

Some countries have annual chocolate exhibitions, although Britain is not one of these.

FRANCE

SALON DU CHOCOLAT
Espace Eiffel-Branly
29-55 Quai Branly
75007 Paris
End of October, beginning of November.

Once a year a shrine to the glory of chocolate is erected opposite the Seine. All the big brand names, specialist chocolatiers, conferences and exhibitions, and a chocolate fashion show.

SWITZERLAND

Hotel Allegro
Schaenzli Strasse 71-77
CH-3000 Bern
Tel: 00413 133 95500
Toblerone created a permanent exhibition to celebrate its 90th birthday in 1998. It takes up three floors of the Hotel Allegro in Bern, Switzerland.

UNITED STATES

CHOCOLATE SHOW
Metropolitan Pavilion
(New York)
Around Thanksgiving time.

Meeting of the Salon du Chocolat in the USA, where European and American chocolatiers show their specialities.

JAPAN

SALON DU CHOCOLAT
Tokyo Forum
Around St Valentine's Day.

A very Japanese gathering devoted to the discovery of chocolate with Japanese and European chocolatiers. Something of a culture shock.

Clubs and associations

BRITAIN

THE CHOCOLATE SOCIETY
Clay Pit Lane
Roecliffe
North Yorkshire YO51 9LS
Tel: 01423 322230
www.chocolate.co.uk
The club has about 3,000 members.

THE CHOCOLATE CLUB
Unit 11
St Pancras Commercial Centre
63 Pratt Street
London NW1 0BY
Tel: 020 7482 8515
Chocolates by mail order; boxes cost from £5.

FRANCE

LE CLUB DES CROQUEURS DE CHOCOLAT
68 *bis* Boulevard Péreire
75017 Paris
The most famous club, with a few VIP members.

LE CLUB DU CHOCOLAT AU PALAIS
62 Rue de Rennes
75006 Paris

Museums

BRITAIN

CADBURY WORLD
London Road
Bournville
Birmingham
Tel: 021 451 4180
www.cadburyworld.co.uk
The museum is situated on the site of the old workers' village, built by the Cadbury family in the 19th century. Life-size models and an 'olde worlde shoppe', take the visitor into a traditionally English world of chocolate.

FRANCE

LE MUSÉE DU CHOCOLAT
14 Avenue Beaurivage
64200 Biarritz
Tel: 00 33 5 59 41 54 64
Maître Couzigou invites you to learn all about chocolate from the 17th century right up to the present. Experience the smells, see the displays, watch the demonstrations.

BELGIUM

MUSEUM OF COCOA AND CHOCOLATE
The House of the Dukes of Brabant
13 Grand Place
B-1000 Brussels
Tel: 00 32 2 514 20 48
Fax: 00 32 2 514 52 05
www.mucc.be
info@mucc.be

GERMANY

THE IMHOFF-STOLLWERCK MUSEUM
Rheinhafen 1a
50678 Cologne
Tel: 00 49 221 931 8880
www.schokoladenmuseum.de
service@www.chokoladenmuseum.de
Visitors will find objects, photographs and many other things associated with chocolate.

CANADA

ÉRICO CHOCO-MUSEUM
634 Rue Saint-Jean
Faubourg Saint-Jean Baptiste
Quebec
Canada G1R 1P8
Tel: 001 418 524 2122
www.chocomusee.com
info@chocomusee.com

Chocolate online

Facts, figures and advertising centred on After Eight mints.

www.aftereight.co.uk

Company website for this French manufacturer.

www.barry-callebaut.com

A British trade asscciation, the Biscuit, Cake, Chocolate and Confectionery Alliance, with a site offering useful facts and figures.

www.bccca.org.uk

A highly informative site about Cadbury products, the company's history, and the history of chocolate generally.

www.cadbury.co.uk

A wealth of information about cocoa.

www.choco-club.com

The American address for chocolate on-line.

www.chocoholic.com

A Swiss site, with text in English. Interesting facts and figures about the history of chocolate.

www.chocolat.ch

Plenty of links worldwide on this site for chocaholics.

www.chocolate.scream.org

Mail-order chocolates from America, and useful links.

www.ChocolatEpicure.com

A site including interesting chocolate trivia.

www.chocolate-guide.com

The famous Belgian brand with the elephant logo. Text in English.

www.cotedor.be

A site for fans of the KitKat.

www.kitkat.co.uk

All you need to know about the American inventor of the filled chocolate bar.

www.mars.com

Information, recipes, dietary advice from Nestle.

www.nestle.co.uk

A dark, seductively designed site with recipes, a little history and pedigrees of 'Grands Chocolates' such as Valrhona.

www.valrhona.com

www.godiva.com

www.lindt.com

Drool over close-up pictures of these famous Belgian pralines.

www.leonidas.be

www.toblerone.com

BUYING CHOCOLATE ONLINE

Free delivery to UK addresses. There's plenty of choice, with products aimed at every type of personality, from the 'cool teenager' to the 'gentleman'.

www.chocexpress.com

This is where to go for UK deliveries of Leonidas chocolates, pralines, Turkish delight, marzipan and truffles.

www.giftstore.co.uk

Chocolatier Hudson Gray produces a range of tempting chocolate products that can be purchased online at this address.

www.chocolates-online.co.uk

This firm, which is over 100 years old, is based in Great Yarmouth. They specialise in making Belgian-style, Continental-style and English milk chocolates – as well as personalized rock candy.

www.handmadechocolates.co.uk

Sweet Seductions sells top quality chocolates and confectionery from around the world, online and from its shop in Leamington Spa.

www.sweet-seductions.co.uk

French chocolates from people who believe that the best are created in France. Their collections have names such as 'sagesse' and 'rêverie'. Website in French and English.

www.zchocolat.com

An American company with stores all over the USA. Purchase online for a taste of their **Venezuelan single bean** chocolate.

www.chocolates-elrey.com

Further reading

Joel Glenn Brenner, *The Emperors of Chocolate: Inside the Secret World of Hershey and Mars*, Random House, 1999

Sophie D. Coe and Michael D. Coe, *The True History of Chocolate*, Thames and Hudson, 1996

Roald Dahl, *Charlie and the Chocolate Factory*, Puffin Books, 1973

Laura Esquivel, *Like Water for Chocolate*, Black Swan, 1993

Joanne Harris, *Chocolat*, Doubleday 1999

Ian Knight, ed., *Chocolate and Cocoa: Health and Nutrition*, Blackwell Science, 1999

Helena Rubinstein, *The Chocolate Book*, Macdonald, 1981

James Runcie, *The Discovery of Chocolate*, HarperCollins, 2001

Delia Smith, *Comic Relief, Delia's Chocolate Collection*, New Crane Publishing, 2001

Christian Teubner, *The Chocolate Bible*, Penguin Studio, 1997

ANANDAMIDE

A neurotransmitter with a similar effect to cannabis, giving a feeling of euphoria.

ARRIBA

A cocoa blend from Ecuador, having a floral aroma with notes of jasmine.

ASSORTED CHOCOLATES

Tender, bite-size chocolates consisting of ganache, praline, marzipan... covered in a fine film of liquid chocolate.

BICERIN

An Italian speciality; a paste made from cocoa, honey and hazelnuts, often used in coffee to replace sugar.

CACAO POD

Fruit of the cacao tree shaped like a small rugby ball. Its hard shell, which changes in colour from yellow to browny-orange when ripe, protects the cacao seeds. It is only the seeds that are used in cocoa production.

CAULIFLORY

A rare characteristic of the cacao tree, whereby the buds, flowers and fruits grow directly out of the trunk and main branches.

CHOCOLATE

The food, the drink and the principal ingredient in chocolate-based foods. It can be plain (cocoa, cocoa butter and sugar), milk (cocoa, cocoa butter, sugar and milk) or white (cocoa butter, sugar and milk). Available in solid block form, chocolate confectionery, chocolate bars, cocoa powder and drinking chocolate powder, chocolate spreads and couverture chocolate.

CHOCOLATE POT

Similar to a coffee pot, this vessel was shaped like a bulb towards the base, with a spout for pouring and a horizontal handle. The lid had an aperture for inserting a stick or whisk to stir the chocolate.

COCOA

Fermented and dried seeds of the cacao tree, also known as raw cocoa or commercial cocoa. Cocoa is divided into two categories: standard cocoa and fine cocoa. The former comes from the forestero variety and is used to make chocolates and chocolate blends. The latter is produced from criollo and trinitario varieties and is used to make premium quality chocolate.

COCOA BEANS

The seeds from the cacao tree are called cocoa beans after fermentation and drying.

COCOA BUTTER

This is the fat obtained by separation from the dry cocoa solids. Cocoa butter is in liquid form after it has been extracted in a hydraulic press. To render it a saleable commodity it is purified to eliminate odours, tempered and moulded into blocks. To make chocolate it is reincorporated into the cocoa mass – which already contains some cocoa butter – to improve the gloss and smoothness of the product. Pharmaceutical and cosmetic companies also make use of it. Ever since Mayan times it has been known that cocoa butter can soothe sunburn. It can also heal burns and chapped skin.

COCOA LIQUOR

Another name for cocoa mass.

COCOA MASS

The cocoa nibs are passed through a succession of grinding cylinders. Subjected to pressure and heat, the cocoa butter contained in the nibs liquefies, resulting in paste with a strong bitter taste known as cocoa mass. Cocoa mass can also be called cocoa liquor.

COCOA POWDER

The result of pulverizing the compressed cocoa cake (that is, the dry cocoa solids) after the extraction of cocoa butter.

CONCHING

This process, invented by Rodolf Lindt in 1879, is a key stage in chocolate making. The cocoa mass, to which cocoa butter has been added, is aerated by gentle heating and kneading, and the chocolate acquires its velvety consistency.

COUVERTURE

The key ingredient used by confectioners and specialist chocolate-makers. It is a mixture of cocoa mass, cocoa butter and sugar (and also milk and almonds according to individual recipes).

CRIOLLO

The original type of cacao tree, producing the most expensive beans, with the best and richest flavour.

CRU

Also known as grand cru, and 100 per cent pure, 'cru' denotes chocolate made from cocoa beans from a single origin (Ecuador, Caribbean, Sri Lanka).

DUTCHING

A process introduced by van Houten to neutralise the acid taste of chocolate and make it more digestible. He used potash, but today a solution such as potassium carbonate is used.

ENROBING

Usually the film of chocolate that coats assorted chocolates. Can also refer to a chocolate moulding.

FILLING

Found inside a chocolate speciality – for example praline inside an assorted chocolate, coconut fondant inside a chocolate bar.

FORESTERO

The most common type of cacao tree, producing cocoa with a less fine flavour than the criollo.

GANACHE

A perfect complement to cocoa, enabling the full appreciation of its strong, aromatic flavours.

A blend of chocolate shavings to which has been added simmered, but not boiled, fresh cream (plain, or flavoured with spices, citrus peel, tea etc.). Used in cakes, handmade chocolates and truffles.

GIANDUJA

Italian praline. A combination of chocolate, roasted and finely ground nuts and icing sugar.

GRAN COUVA

A hot and fruity cocoa blend from a single plantation on Trinidad.

MOLE POBLANO

A rich sauce containing chocolate, fruit and nuts, supposedly invented by the nuns of the Santa Roas convent in Puebla, Mexico, in honour of a visiting archbishop. However, the recipe is probably older, and a version of this sauce was said to have been served to the Aztec king Montezuma.

MOULDED CHOCOLATE

The term used to describe couverture chocolate poured into thermo formed plastic moulds to produce an array of Easter eggs, chocolate bells, Father Christmas figures etc.

NIBS

Dried, roasted, and roughly crushed cocoa beans.

ORIGIN

Determines the flavour and final quality.

PHENYLETHYLAMINE

A stimulant found in chocolate; along with theobromine; it has an antidepressant effect.

POLYPHENOLS

A group of chemicals found in chocolate, which include antioxidants.

PRALINE

A filling for chocolates, made with almonds (or other nuts) and sugar.

SACHERTORTE

A cake made with chocolate and apricot preserve, reputedly originating in the Sacher Hotel in Vienna.

SALSOLINOL

An alkaloid that has an antidepressant effect; it is found in chocolate.

SOYA LECITHIN

This emulsifier is permitted in chocolate manufacture. It is added at conching (last stage in the manufacturing process). It helps to improve the texture of chocolate, improving the gloss and snap by stabilising the fats.

TEMPERING

The controlled reduction in temperature of chocolate to produce the required consistency.

THEOBROMINE

A stimulant found in chocolate.

TRINITARIO

A type of cacao tree produced by crossing the criollo and the forestero varieties.

TRUFFLE

Ganache that has been rolled in cocoa powder and icing sugar.

Contents

Fact ⟫ 2–12
Fun facts and quick quotes

Discover ⟫ 13–46

Look ⟫ 47–64
Posters advertising chocolate from around the world

In practice ⟫ 65–98

Find out ⟫ 99–125

Picture credits

P.14, American museum, Madrid, Artephot (Oronoz) **–P.16,** American museum, Madrid, Artephot (Oronoz) **–P.19,** Engraving by G. Gallina in 'Ancient or modern costume of Jules Ferrario', Milan, 1820, Decorative Arts Library, Paris, Jean-Loup Charnet **–P.20,** Silk lampas, Carnavalet museum, Paris, Lauros-Giraudon **–P.23,** Maritime museum, RMN **–P.24,** O'Shea Gallery, London, The Bridgeman Art Library **–P.27,** Watercolour by Jan Van Grevenbroek II, Correr museum, Venice, Giraudon **–P.28,** Jean-Loup Charnet **–P.31,** Jean-Loup Charnet **–P.32,** Painting by Albert Guillaume, Hachette Photolibrary **–P.35,** Artephot (Oronoz) **–P.36,** Kharbine-Tapabor **–P.39,** Kharbine-Tapabor **–P.40,** Corbis (Brett) **–P.43,** Watercolour from manuscript collection on plants of the Antilles at the end of the 17th century, Jean-Loup Charnet **-P.43,** Culinary Photolibrary **–P.48-49,** Sendraf, 1937, publicity museum **–P.50,** Sir William Nicholson, The Bridgeman Art Library **–P.51,** 19th century, The Bridgeman Art Library **–P.52,** Firmin Bouisset, 1895, publicity museum **–P.53,** Retrographic Archive Ltd **–P.54-55,** German school, 19th century, The Bridgeman Art Library **–P.56,** Hachette Photolibrary **–P.57,** Retrographic Archive Ltd **–P.58,** Hervé Morvan, publicity museum **–P.59,** Swiss school, 19th century, The Bridgeman Art Library **–P.60,** Charles Loupot, 1926, publicity museum **–P.61,** MJ between 1885 and 1890, publicity museum **–P.62,** A. Cornetti, 1920, publicity museum **–P.63,** Retrographic Archive Ltd **–P.64,** Etienne Boucher, publicity museum **–P.66-79,** Jsi* **–P.80-94,** Phare International (Gilbert Necioli) **–P.97,** Top (Jean-François RiviPre) **–P.98,** National Union of chocolatiers **–P.101, 103, 104, 107, 108, 111,** Vincent Gravé **–P.113,** Hachette Photolibrary **–P.114,** Stills Press Agency (Christophe Geral) **–P.115,** Explorer (Lausat collection) **–P.116-119,** Vincent Grav **–P.122, 125,** Vincent Gravé.

Acknowledgements

The author and editor thank all those who were kind enough to answer their questions and supply the information necessary for this book.
In particular, we express our thanks to Michel Barel of Cirad; Sylvie Douce, founder of the Salon du Chocolat; Stéphane Bonnat, chocolatier at Voiron (IsPre); Sylvain Margou, general secretary of the National Union of chocolatiers; Jean Colaneri, general secretary of the Club des croqueurs du chocolat; Irène Frain, writer, and member of the Club des croqueurs de chocolat; Valrhona in Tain-l'Hermitage.